Praise for this

"This fast moving book gives a proven, practical approach that you can learn and apply immediately to start a successful business, or to build your current business into a lean, mean profit machine."

BRIAN TRACY, success guru, speaker and author, "*Now, Build a Great Business!*"

"Bite-sized strategy for the small businessperson— crisp, concise and easily digested on one plane journey!"

DAVID WILLIAMSON, Managing Partner, Nova Capital Management

"At last! A book on business strategy I can read!"

FIDELIS FERNANDEZ, small businessman

"Strategy in a nutshell, tailor-made for the small businessperson."

JAMES PITT, Partner, Lexington Partners

"Small business owners or managers all know they lack one precious commodity: time. Managing the now often means tomorrow, with strategy put on the back-burner—they know it should be done, but when and how? They have no director of strategy because the business is too small—and when do they have the time to learn about strategy?

KISSTRATEGY helps break that deadlock. Vaughan Evans replaces the heavy theory associated with strategy books with a short, sharp, three stage approach, along with solid examples, tips and charts—and all conveyed in a lively, engaging writing style.

This book is a must-read for the small businessperson. Take it off the shelf, read, apply and profit."

GRAHAME HUGHES, founding director, Haven Power

"If you want to take your startup or small business to the next level, you need a strategy. This can often seem complex—but not so with this little book. Vaughan Evans does what he says on the tin—he Keeps It Simple, Successfully!"

STEPHEN LAWRENCE, CEO, Protocol Education and former Managing Director, Arthur D. Little

"If you want investment, you must have a robust strategy—one which will convince your backer that you can and will grow your business. This book shows you, simply and succinctly, how to do it."

JONATHAN DERRY-EVANS, partner, Manfield Capital Partners

KISSTRATEGY

A KEEP-IT-SIMPLE GUIDE ON HOW TO BUILD A WINNING STRATEGY FOR YOUR STARTUP OR SMALL BUSINESS

VAUGHAN EVANS

Printed in The United States of America by CreateSpace

ISBN: 978-0-9561391-4-6

To all those with the guts, grit
and gumption to run their
own business

Contents

About the author

Vaughan Evans is an independent consultant in business strategy and planning. He worked formerly at investment bankers Bankers Trust Co and for many years at Cambridge, Massachusetts-based management and technology consultants Arthur D. Little.

He is the author of many successful books on business strategy and planning, including the best-selling *Key Strategy Tools* (Pearson, 2012) and, with success guru Brian Tracy, *The Standout Business Plan: Make It Irresistible and Get the Funds You Need for Your Startup or Growing Business* (AMACOM, 2014).

Vaughan is also a charismatic and enthralling speaker and seminar leader. His keynote speech on *KISSTRATEGY*, how to keep business strategy simple, yet backable, is as instructive as it is entertaining. He is the author of the pithy, witty yet educational *Stand, Speak, Deliver!: How to Survive – and Thrive – in Public Speaking and Presenting* (Little Brown, 2015).

For advice on strategy or planning for your business, please contact him directly via his website: www.vaughanevansandpartners.com

Preface

I have written a number of books on business strategy and planning. They have sold quite well and received largely positive feedback from entrepreneurs and managers, as well as financiers, consultants, and professors. I prided myself that I managed to make often tricky concepts accessible to owners and managers of businesses large and small.

I may have been wrong.

I asked an old friend, a small businessman, for his feedback on one such book, the shortest and most straightforward I had written to that date and one aimed at small businesspeople and middle managers.

This was his response:

> "Barring the odd exception, I doubt if any would-be entrepreneur would commit the time to read it. It is too long—it takes longer than one hour to read. Your book is far too technical and demanding for a layman. He has other needs for his time."

That hurt. The very person I had in mind when writing the book wouldn't read it!

But his rather brutal critique spurred me to write this book. It is unashamedly for him, for entrepreneurs and managers of small businesses who have very little time to read a business book—and when they do they want the message conveyed as plainly and as quickly as possible.

KISSTRATEGY does what it says on the tin. It keeps strategy simple.

It cuts strategy to the quick—the very essence of what you

need to know to draw up a strategy for your small business.

It is as light on the theory as is possible, while still conveying the message.

It strives to be jargon-free.

It illustrates each section with well known examples from the world of business.

Where possible, it uses charts rather than words—streamlining the message.

Above all, it is short—and readable in an hour, on one train or plane journey.

This book is for you, my old friend.

Enjoy!

Introduction

Simplicity is the ultimate sophistication",

Leonardo da Vinci

In this introduction

- On KISSTRATEGY
- Getting ready—knowing your business
- Getting ready—taking aim

On KISSTRATEGY

First things first. Why should you, an entrepreneur or manager of a small business, draw up a strategy? What is it? Why does your firm need it?

The answer is simple. Strategy is what you need to get your firm from where you are today to where to want to be in a few years' time.

But, you might say, why do I need a strategy to do that? The firm can just carry on what it is doing now, maybe introduce a new product here, enter a new market there and in three years' time we should have larger profits than what we have today.

Fine. You have a strategy. It's called 'seat-of-the-pants'. Your firm is at the mercy of the market. If demand takes a dip, or if customers switch to a substitute offering, your revenues will tumble. Likewise if a competitor comes up with a superior product or radically improves standards of service.

And what if you launch a new product which is super but fails to excite your customers?

The market may remain favorable. You may make the right investment calls. You may achieve your hoped-for profits in Year 3. But that's called luck.

Strategy is about reducing dependence on luck.

It's about guiding your company to the next level—while recognizing what is happening in the market, making the most of your company's capabilities and managing risk to acceptable levels.

More specifically, and in business jargon, just this once, strategy is about how you deploy your firm's scarce resources to develop an enduring competitive advantage—and thereby achieve your goals and objectives.

Every company, from the corner tire repair shop to Apple Inc., needs a strategy. Without one, you'll be floating on a wing and a prayer.

With a strategy, you have a better chance of getting to where you want to go.

And the good news is that it doesn't have to be that complex to draw one up.

It was the US Navy in the 1960s that reportedly coined the KISS principle. 'Keep It Simple, Stupid' was adopted as the principle on which the design of naval warplanes should be based—for obvious reasons. The simpler the design, the less complex the engineering, the more likely would engineers on aircraft carriers at sea, far from port and sophisticated onshore maintenance facilities, be able to fix problems themselves.

In this book I have applied the KISS principle to strategy development. I looked at the Strategy Pyramid approach I developed in earlier books (see the Appendix) and stripped it back to its bare essentials.

In particular, I strived to reduce the number of parts or components of strategy development to *three*—for this is the number of items that psychologists tell us can be readily related to *and remembered* by the average person.

I found that it was indeed possible. And simple. This is it: developing strategy = understanding the market + creating competitive advantage + managing risk.

Even simpler, leaving out the verbs: Strategy = Market + Advantage + Risk—see Figure 0.1, which unashamedly builds on the kiss theme.

This is strategy kept simple. This is KISSTRATEGY.

The parts are sequential. Understanding the market must come first. It underpins strategy development. It should be the horse to the strategy cart.

Managing risk is the trailer behind the cart. It represents the fine-tuning of strategy.

Figure 0.1 **The three elements of KISSTRATEGY**

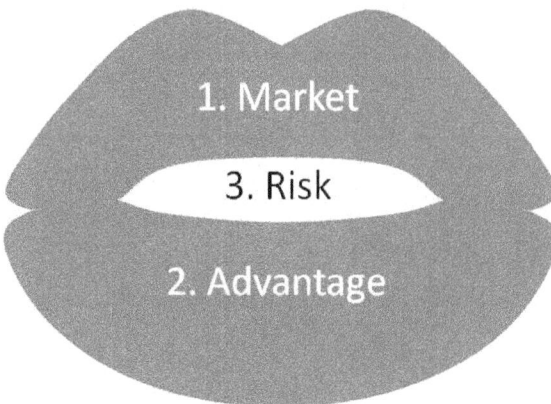

Creating competitive advantage is the cargo on the cart, the essence of strategy.

But before we embark on the first stage, understanding the market, we need to do some preparation. We need to get ready...

Getting ready—knowing your business

Before getting started on your strategy development, pause for a while.

In which cupboards of your business do the profits reside?

You need to know your business. You need to clarify the major business segments you compete in and which contribute most, both to the top line and to the bottom line. Now and in the future.

If your business is a startup, you need to do the same. But we'll start with identifying key segments in an established business.

Identifying key segments

Does your firm serve some segments where you generate good sales but frustratingly little profit? And what of those happier segments where sales are modest but margins meaty?

Step one in strategy development is to know your business, where the profit resides.

There are three components to this:

- Which business segments does your firm compete in—which products* do you sell to which sets of customers?
- Which of these segments delivers the most profit?
- How may this change over time?

* Or services, but we'll call them 'products' too in this section.

KISS tip

Be careful of paralysis through analysis. Don't end up with dozens of segments. Concentrate on the half-dozen or so that truly drive your firm's operating profit.

Only once you have completed this segmentation should you embark on developing your strategy. There is no point devoting hours of research, whether in analyzing competitor data or gathering customer feedback, on a segment which contributes to just 1% of your operating profit—and which offers little prospect of growing that contribution over the next five years.

How you could strengthen your capabilities in that segment may be fascinating, but is not material to your business strategy and of little interest to your board or backer.

You need to devote your time and effort to strengthening your firm's presence in those segments that contribute, or will contribute, to 80% or more of your business.

First, then, what is your business mix? What products or services does your business sell and to which customer groups?

Which count for most in your business?

Businesses seldom offer just the one product to one customer group. Most businesses offer a number of distinct products to a number of distinct customer groups, reachable through differing marketing approaches.

Each distinct product offered to a distinct customer group is a segment.

Which segments contribute most to your firm's sales?

How has the contribution of key segments to sales changed over the last few years? And how may it change over the next few years?

You may find it helpful to present that data in a pie chart, as for example in Figure 0.2.

Figure 0.2 **Business mix**

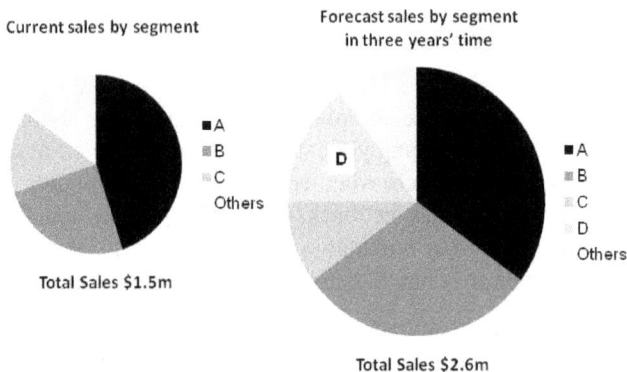

Current sales by segment

Forecast sales by segment
in three years' time

Total Sales $1.5m

Total Sales $2.6m

And what about profit? Which segments contribute most to gross profit? And, if you have the data, or you can make reasonable estimates of the breakdown of overheads, which contribute most to operating profit?

How has the contribution of key segments to operating profit changed over the last few years? And how may it change over the next few years?

Pop the profit data by segment into another couple of pie charts and compare with those for revenue. What does that tell you?

This segmentation analysis will give you the base understanding of your business upon which to develop your strategy.

Segmentation in a startup

If you are starting a new venture, you may still need to segment—unless you are launching just the one product (or service) to one group of customers.

Apple's sensational segments

What will be the next Apple blockbuster product? Will there be one?

In the 1990s Apple was a manufacturer of personal computers, one with a devoted following, but not large enough to prevent it from struggling financially. Sales stared to decline in 1995 and were not to reach those levels again until 2005, during which time it recorded either low or negative profitability.

Yet Apple went on to become the most valuable company in history, topping $750 billion in 2015. How did that happen?

A segmentation of Apple's business in the late 1990s would have shown a broad range of Macintosh personal computers, categorized perhaps by product, user type and region. The PCs were facing tough competition from IBM and its many clones, now with an improved graphical user interface and running a superior operating system, Microsoft. Market share was eroding.

One new segment showed promise—a personal digital assistant, the Newton. Another was even more embryonic—a portable digital audio player, to be called the iPod, linking it to the promising flashy redesign of the Macintosh, the iMac.

The iPod turned the tide and lead to iTunes, a revolution in music industry online distribution. Then came the iPhone, a device which blended stylistically the capabilities of mobile phone, digital audio/video player, and digital camera. Later Apple launched the iPad, a tablet computer which seemed destined to cannibalize other lines but succeeded in creating its own category.

Personal computers now comprise just 10% of Apple's sales (Q2, 2016). Two thirds of sales come from the iPhone and related products and services, which have largely cannibalized the iPod (down to 4%).

> Drawing up Apple's strategy for the next few years will not be easy. How to withstand competition from Samsung, HTC, and others in the smartphone market will be tough enough, but what about the next big thing?
>
> Apple's strategists will need to take extra care with segmentation. Which product will be the next iPod? An iPhantastic challenge.

But are you sure you'll only have just the one product? Or one customer group?

Try categorizing your products. And your customers. Is further segmentation meaningful? If so, use it. If not, don't waste time just for the sake of seeming serious. Stick to the one product for the one customer group, i.e. one business segment.

But there is one big difference in a startup. No matter how you segment, no matter how many customer groups you identify, they are all, at present, gleams in the eye.

You have no customers. Yet.

Your product must be couched in terms of its benefits to the customer. That is the business proposition.

Not the way in which your product can do this, do that, at this price. But the way in which your product or service can *benefit* the target customer.

Who is the target customer? In which way will he or she benefit from your offering?

And that is just in the one segment. Are there others?

Segmentation may lie at the very heart of your business proposition. It may have been how you unearthed a niche where only your offering can yield benefit to the customer.

For further stimulating thoughts on this, see the section on 'Will the fish bite?' in John Mullins' indispensable guide to business startups, *The New Business Road Test: What Entrepreneurs and Executives Should Do Before Writing a Business*

Plan.

Here is a slightly different way of looking at it. Does your offering address some 'unmet need' in the marketplace? Does it fill a gap in a target customer's needs? This is one of the secrets to a new venture's success highlighted by William Bridges in his book, *Creating You & Co.* He suggests that an 'unmet need' could be uncovered by spotting signs such as a missing piece in a pattern, an unrecognized opportunity, an underused resource, a signal event, an unacknowledged change, a supposedly impossible situation, a nonexistent but needed service, a new or emerging problem, a bottleneck, an interface, or other similar signs.

However you define the customer benefit, whether in terms of an unmet need or in a way more meaningful to your offering, you need to undertake some basic research to dig up whatever evidence you can glean of likely customer benefit.

This may help you clarify segmentation in your startup.

Getting ready—taking aim

Where do you want your business to be in three to five years' time? What sort of a firm do you want it to be? On which parameters will you measure performance success?

What are the aims of your firm?

There are numerous treatises written on the relative merits of a company articulating its vision, mission, aims, purposes, goals, objectives, values, principles, ideals, beliefs, principles and so on. The sound of hair splitting can be deafening.

It is simpler and adequate to stick to two of these: goals and objectives.

A goal is something your business aims to be, as described in words. An objective is a target that helps to measure whether that goal is achieved, and is typically set out in numbers.

One of your goals may be for your business to be the most customer-centric provider of your services in your state. Objectives to back up that goal could be the achievement of a

> **KISS tip**
>
> Should your over-riding goal be maximizing share-
> holder value in your company? To what extent should
> you also be striving to serve the interests of other
> stakeholders, such as employees, customers, the com-
> munity, the environment?
>
> It is your call. There is an inescapable trade-off. But
> remember that without shareholder value you have no
> business. And that would benefit no one—not you,
> your employees, your customers, not even the tax-
> man—other than your competitors.

'highly satisfied' rating of 30% from your annual customer
survey by 2017 and 35% by 2019, along with 80% 'satisfied'
or better by that year.

Goals are directional, objectives are specific. The former
should look beyond the short-term and set out where you see
the firm in the long term. The latter should be 'SMART',
namely Specific, Measurable, Attainable, Relevant, and Time-
limited—see later in this section.

The setting of long-term goals and SMART objectives are essential tools in strategy development.

Setting long-term goals

Goal setting is at the cornerstone of business strategy. Goals
should underpin each of your company's main strategic initiatives over the next five years or so.

Here are three considerations when setting goals:

- Goals differ from objectives.

- Goals should be long-term—short-term goals have little
  place in strategy development.

- The best goals are also motivational.

Figure 0.2 **Setting long-term goals**

A goal is something your business aims to be, as described in words. An objective is a target that helps to measure whether that goal is achieved, and is typically set out in numbers. Your goal may be to become a low cost provider in a key segment. An accompanying objective might be to reduce unit operating costs in that segment within three years by 15%.

Second, think of short-term goals as what lies within and behind this year's budget. These may be important in the short-

---

KISS tip

Don't have too many goals. They say people can't remember more than three of any list, but you may choose to stretch that to four or five.

Go for a dozen and you'll be lucky to attain half of them. Go for a handful and you may bag the lot.

Life at Mars

What Hoover is to the vacuum cleaner market, so too Mars in choc bars—virtually a generic term.

Yet there is much more to Mars Inc than its eponymous choc bar. It was not even its launch product—that was the Milky Way bar. Many people don't even know that Milky Way belongs to Mars Inc, let alone M&Ms.

Most are also unaware that chocolate confectionery is but one slice of a huge, low key, private company, turning over $33 billion and employing 75,000, with six strategic business units—chocolate, petcare, chewing gum, food, drink, and life sciences, despite these units selling such well known international brands as Pedigree Chum, Wrigley gum, and Uncle Ben's.

That is because Mars Inc remains a privately owned— and private—company. There are shades of its founders, father Frank and son Forrest Mars, in the company's five core principles of doing business:

- Quality—the consumer is our boss...

- Responsibility—as individuals, we demand total responsibility from ourselves...

- Mutuality—our actions should never be at the expense of others...

- Efficiency—we use resources to the full and waste nothing...

- Freedom—we need freedom to shape our future...

Mars Inc believes that these principles are 'a set of fundamental beliefs that help to shape and define us as a company; they express our vision not only of who we are, but where and what we want to be'.

This is all worthy stuff and perhaps these principles genuinely serve to motivate employees. But try stating some opposites or antonyms against key words, for example:

- Quality—the consumer is our servant...

- Responsibility—we demand no responsibility from ourselves...

- Mutuality—our actions should always be at the expense of others...

- Efficiency—we waste everything...

- Freedom—we need captivity to shape our future...

A company with such principles wouldn't survive too long, implying that those of Mars Inc are self-evident. They represent motherhood and apple pie. Unlike goals and objectives, they are of little use for purposes of strategy development.

But these principles seem to work for Mars Inc. And there may be lessons for others in this proselytizing approach to business.

term, whether for keeping the financial markets or your owners happy or for you landing that performance-related bonus.

But what lies within that budget may have little impact on strategy development. Strategy takes into account market demand trends and industry competition forces that go well beyond the short term. It is no good gearing up your business to compete ferociously in the short-term only to be exposed to a drop-off in demand or reduced competitiveness in the medium to long term.

Third, goal setting should also prove motivational. Market or customer-oriented goals are often the most motivational for the sales force and easy enough to monitor. Market share data is readily collected by companies beyond a certain size. A goal could be market leadership in a particular segment within three years.

Customer satisfaction or retention goals (or objectives—see the next tool) can also have the same effect. Operational goals are also incentivizing for the operations team—and even simpler to monitor than market-related goals.

Setting SMART objectives

Objectives are intimately linked to goals. Your firm aims towards a goal, a destination typically articulated in words. Objectives are targets, whether along the route or at the final destination, and are typically set out in numbers.

You may aim for the goal of Ohio state market leadership in a key segment by 2019. That is a worthy goal, but a bit too vague for a robust strategy. More precise would be the corresponding objectives of attaining 33% market share by 2017 and 35% by 2019. This objective should help deliver your goal of market leadership in that segment.

KISS tip

Here is another take on the same theme. Richard Rumelt, in his best-selling book of 2011, Good Strategy, Bad Strategy, states that strategy implementation is greatly assisted by the identification of 'proximate objectives'. Each of these is a target that is close enough that the firm 'can reasonably be expected to hit, or even overwhelm it'. He is emphasizing the attainable ('A') component of a SMART objective.

He cites the example of President Kennedy pledging to place a man on the moon. The objective sounded fanciful, but it conveyed ambition. And Kennedy had an ace up his sleeve—he knew the technology already existed for such a mission to succeed.

Figure 0.3   **Setting SMART objectives**

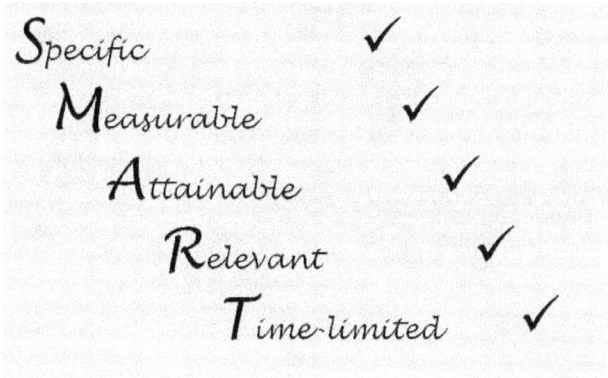

Specific ✓
Measurable ✓
Attainable ✓
Relevant ✓
Time-limited ✓

Whereas goals are indicative and directional, objectives are precise. You should set objectives that are:

- *Specific*—a precise number against a particular parameter.

- *Measurable*—that parameter must be quantifiable—for example, a market share percentage in a segment rather than a woolly target such as 'best supplier'.

- *Attainable*—there is no point in aiming for the improbable—disappointment will be the inevitable outcome.

- *Relevant*—the objective should relate to the goal; if the goal is market leadership, an objective of winning 'best marketing campaign of the year' in the trade journal would be inappropriate.

- *Time-limited*—you should specify by when the objective should be achieved; an objective with no time limitation would serve no motivational purpose and result in the slippage of difficult decisions.

Objectives should be *S-M-A-R-T*—see Figure 0.2. The best objectives are indeed smart. As in the Ohio example above, the objectives are: *Specific* (a market share target in that segment), *Measurable* (market research to which you subscribe will reveal whether the 35% is met), *Attainable* (you are at 29% now and your new product range has been well received), *Relevant* (market share is the ultimate measure of market leadership), and *Time-limited* (2019).

As with goal setting, keep it simple. One or two objectives against each of 4 to 5 goals should be fine.

Ok, you've segmented your business and you've set your long-term goals and SMART objectives.

You're ready for KISSTRATEGY...

1 Under-standing the market

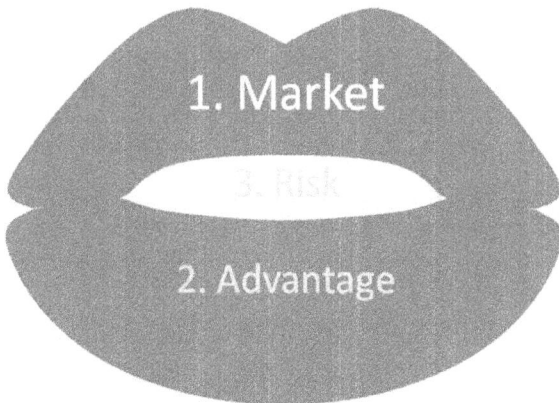

\\\

Time spent on reconnaissance is seldom wasted, military maxim

In this chapter

- Assessing market demand
- Assessing industry competition

The market lies at the bedrock of strategy. A strategy that is built upon a solid understanding of the market is like a house built on a concrete foundation.

A strategy that is premised on how wonderful your business offering is, and hang the market, is like a house built on sand. It will be washed away.

To paraphrase the famous military maxim, time spent on reconnaissance—on reconnoitring the market—is seldom wasted.

There are two sides of the market which need to be tackled: demand and supply.

The supply side deals with production and the forces driving competition between the producers, thus determining outcomes such as market share, pricing, and profitability.

But let's start with the demand side—how to size market demand and how to forecast where it is headed.

Assessing market demand

"It's better to have the wind at your back than in your face", unattributed.

How big is the market your firm is addressing? What factors have been influencing demand growth? How are these factors changing? By how much will demand grow in the future? What are the risks?

These are the questions you need answers to—and you need to answer them for each of your main business segments.

Sizing the market

Size is important.

Without market size you may find it hard to gauge market demand growth. And you certainly won't know market share. Without market share, it's hard to judge competitive position. Then you may find it hard to draw up a winning strategy.

The larger your company, the easier it is to find data on market size. Industry associations proliferate and many either compute market share themselves or contract out the job to specialist market research firms. The latter compete fiercely with one other to cover each and every market where they perceive there to be a sufficient number of customers to turn a profit.

SMEs don't enjoy such lavish attention from market research firms. Some do, and I am often pleasantly surprised when a client turning over $10-20 million reveals monthly market data provided to the firm and its half dozen competitors by some enterprising market researcher, often a one-man band.

Most SMEs don't have access to market data. And they are not alone. A medium-sized firm turning over $100 million may well have the bulk of its business covered by market research reports, but not necessarily that star business segment turning over $8 million, with only two main competitors and growing at 25%/year. That segment may as yet be too small with too few potential customers to entice a market researcher.

Where no data on market size can be found off the shelf, you should try to size the market yourself. One of the best ways to do this is through 'marketcrafting'—estimating the size (in turnover or employees, whatever works best) of each of your

main competitors in relation to yours. Add them all up, make
an allowance for other smaller competitors, and there's your
estimate of market size.

Marketcrafting is hardly an accurate process, nor can it be
guaranteed that the final number will not be some way out.
But it is better than nothing, because you can now use the results to get values of three parameters key to strategy development:

- Market growth—repeat the marketcrafting exercise
  to estimate the market size of three years ago (in
  relation to the size of your business three years
  ago); you now have two data points, hence you can
  derive an estimate of recent market growth.

- Market share—now you 'know' market size, you
  also know your market share (your level of sales
  divided by estimated market size); you also have
  estimated market share of each of your competitors.

- Best of all, market share change—you have your
  market share of today and that of three years ago, so
  you have an estimate of your market share gain (or
  loss), as well as for each of your competitors; these
  estimates will be most useful in assessing your
  competitive position later on.

Marketcrafting sets you up neatly for what is to come.

Forecasting market demand

The quote at the beginning of this section, about it being better
to have the wind at your back than in your face, is one that is
often heard in the business world.

It's a question of odds. You have a better chance of prospering
in a market that's growing than one that's shrinking.

Market size is all very well, but what often matters more in
strategy development is what the market is doing, where it is
going—the dynamics, as opposed to the statics. Is market de-

KISS tip

Treat the marketcrafting results with caution. If your analysis suggests a competitor has a market share of 24% and you hear that their sales director has been boasting that his company has a third of the market at a recent trade show, don't dismiss it off hand as sales spiel. Take another look at your numbers.

Is there any way the braggart could be right? Does he have access to information that you don't? What would his estimate imply for your share, or other competitors' shares?

The numbers are rough, very rough, and need cross-checking at every opportunity. But they are better than nothing and seldom misleading.

mand in your main business segments growing, shrinking, or flat-lining?

This is the big question. It's not the only one, of course. Equally important, as we'll see later on, is the nature of the competition you face and how you're placed to compete. But it's the first big question.

I developed many years ago a four-step process for translating market demand trends and drivers into forecasts. I call it the HOOF approach, for two reasons. HDDF, the strict representation of the first letters in each of the four steps, would be an unattractive, unmemorable acronym—but, with the appropriate creative license, the circular O can be borrowed as a lookalike to the semi-circular D!

And also because it reminds me fondly of the junior soccer team I used to coach. No matter how many times I screeched at a couple of players to play the simple ball out of defense, head up, along the ground, to a nearby player, they would blindly HOOF it down the pitch with all their might, as far as their adolescent muscles could propel it!

There are four distinct stages in the HOOF approach to demand forecasting. Get this process right and all falls logically into place. Get it out of step and you may end up with a misleading answer. You need to apply these steps for each of your main business segments.

The four steps are:

- *Historic growth*—assess how market demand has grown in the past, using data either from market research or from your own marketcrafting exercise (see above).

- *Drivers past*—identify what has been driving that past growth, for example per capita income growth, specific population growth, technological change, Government policy, changing awareness, pricing shifts, fashion, customer sector growth.

- *Drivers future*—assess whether there will be any change in influence of these and other drivers in the future, especially in relation to the economic cycle.

- *Forecast growth*—forecast market demand growth, based on the influence of future drivers and relying as much on judgment as on numbers.

Let's take a simple example of the HOOF approach in action. In one of your business segments, your firm offers a relatively new service to the elderly. Step 1 (H): You find that the market has been growing at 5-10% per year over the last few years. Step 2 (O): You identify the main drivers as (a) per capita income growth, (b) growth in the elderly population, and (c) growing awareness of the service by elderly people. Step 3 (O): You believe income growth will continue as before, the elderly population will grow even faster in the future, and that awareness can only get more widespread. Step 4 (F): You conclude that growth in your market will accelerate and could reach over 10% per year over the next few years.

You may find it helpful to use the HOOF approach in chart form—see Figure 1.1 for the above example of a service to the

Figure 1.1 The HOOF approach to demand forecasting: an example

Demand drivers for a new service for the elderly	Impact on demand growth		
	Recent past	Now	Next few years
Growth in incomes	-	o	+
Growth in elderly population	+	+	++
Increased awareness of service	++	++	+++
Overall impact	+	+	++
Market growth rate	5 to 10%/yr	5 to 10%	>10%/yr

Key to driver impact
+ Positive o None - Negative

H **D** **D** **F**

elderly.

Assessing demand for a startup

If your business is a startup, this may well be the trickiest part of your strategy development. And the most crucial.

Yours may be a new product or service designed to convey a customer benefit not previously realizable. In which case, how do you define the market?

What is market demand for a product that has not previously existed? What is its size? What are its growth prospects?

On the other hand, your startup may be in a market that's already well defined—like a guest house, which may well be unique and distinctive, but fits snugly into an already buoyant market for three star tourism in your region.

Or you may be opening a boutique selling designer children-swear on Main Street. Again that is a definable, existing mar-

No wrap for the movie theater

How many times have we heard of the death knell for the movie theater over the last few decades?

Sure their hey-day was far distant, in the 1930s and 40s. The equivalent of one half of the US population went to watch *Gone with the Wind*. Theaters were not expected to survive the onslaught of the television in the 1950s, which turned everyone's living room into a mini-theater, but they did.

Then along came the video-recorder, cable TV, the DVD player, satellite TV, the internet, gaming consoles, home entertainment systems, broadband, video-on-demand... and yet the movie theater survives.

And even thrives. Look at the numbers: US box office admissions per capita averaged 4-5 times a year in the mid-1960s—and still do! There have been plenty of annual fluctuations, with peaks reflecting factors such as the arrival of multiplexes, and later megaplexes, or of blockbusters, starting with Jaws in the mid-1970s and continued ever since by superheroes, or of 3D movies.

Troughs have reflected technological advance in home entertainment systems as well as the huge improvement in the quality and addictiveness of product on TV channels, from series such as *The Wire* to *Homeland*, *Game of Thrones* and *Breaking Bad*.

Meanwhile prices have gone up, reflecting to some extent the transformation of movie theaters from the flea pits of the post-war period to the plush settings of today.

If at any time in the last 50 years you had been tasked to forecast market demand in the movie theater business, you would have had to take into account a whole host of demand drivers, not just the obvious. Not just technological advance in home entertainment, not just physical, technological or content advance in cinematic

> experience, but lifestyle changes too—including the need for people, especially the young, to socialize, to enjoy a group experience, to be able to participate in discussion around the water cooler.
>
> All demand drivers, whether measurable or not, need to be factored into any forecast. As for the movie theater industry, one thing remains for sure: it will not go with the wind.

ket, to be researched in the same way as set out above.

But what if yours is indeed something that has not existed before? How can you convince your backer that there will be buyers of your product or service, and at that price? You need evidence.

You'll have to do some test marketing. If yours is a business-to-business proposition, get on the phone and set up meetings with prospective corporate buyers. Explain the benefits of your product and why at that price they have a bargain.

Keep a record of these meetings and analyze the findings. Write a report drawing out key conclusions from the discussions, with each supported by bulleted evidence—whether comments from named customers, comments from third parties quoted in the press, data dug up off the web. Collate them into a short and sharp market research report, which will be an appendix to your strategy document.

If yours is a business-to-consumer product or service, test it downtown. Get out your clipboard, stand in a mall or outside a supermarket and talk to shoppers. If you're offering a product, show them. If a service, explain lucidly but swiftly its benefits.

Again, collate the responses, analyze them, draw firm conclusions, support them with quotes and data, and stick the market research report in your appendix.

Now, based on those responses, make an estimate of your potential market size. Imagine there were many suppliers of your product or service and that the whole country is aware of its existence, what would the market size be? How does that compare with the market size for products or services not a million miles different from what you'll be offering? Does your estimate make sense?

And how about market demand growth? If your startup is serving an existing market, then you can use the same HOOF approach for demand forecasting that an established business would use.

If your startup is for a new market, forecasting demand growth will not be your prime consideration. That will be the existence of such a market in the first place. Any growth on top of discovering and serving a new market will be icing on the cake.

KISS tip

If your business is a startup, test the market. Pick up the phone or get out and talk to people. Do some primary market research.

Amass, digest, and analyze pertinent data. Be armed for the inevitable grilling from your backer.

Assessing industry competition

"The trouble with the rat race is that even if you win you are still a rat", Lily Tomlin.

Face it. You are not alone. There are others who offer the same, or very similar, products or services as you.

They are your competition. Pay them due respect. Then outwit them.

But first think about the issues that apply to all of you, to you and to your competitors. These are the issues of industry competition.

This is the other aspect of understanding the market. The first was market demand, covered in the last section. This is the supply side. Market demand and industry competition, demand and supply, together compose the market in which your firm operates.

You need to understand both sides of the market in your KISSTRATEGY development.

In this section we'll look at the supply side in five parts:

- Checking out your competitors.

- Gauging competitive intensity.

- Identifying customer buying criteria.

- Deriving factors for success in your industry—a crucial preparatory step prior to creating a competitive advantage for your firm in Chapter 2.

- Acknowledging competition in a startup

First, take a good look at your competitors.

Checking out your competitors

Who do you compete with? Do you compete with different firms in your different segments? Do you compete indirectly with other firms?

You need to find out all you can about your competitors, in each segment, whether direct or indirect. Pull together any data, info or opinion you can unearth—from the web, trade fairs, suppliers, customers, industry observers, former employees etc— on their sales, sales growth, operating margin (difficult to find if a private company), ownership, segment focus, location of facilities and sales/service teams, physical assets deployed, and, of course, strategy—main focus, positioning, USP, pricing policy, recent investment, growth or repositioning plans—the works.

> **KISS tip**
>
> Research your competitors thoroughly. Remember
> General Sun Tzu's advice: know the enemy.

Next, think on this: just how tough is competition in your industry?

Gauging competitive intensity

Some industries are more competitive than others. Hopefully yours is one which is at the lesser end of the competitiveness spectrum. But you need to know.

One point of clarification: the term 'industry' sometimes conjures up images such as laborers stripped to the waist toiling to shovel coal into furnaces. Not so here. It is used in its broadest context—any group of producers or service providers collectively serving a market for a particular good or service.

There are six main pressures on any industry which together act to determine the intensity of competition (see Figure 1.2):

- *Internal rivalry*—from your competitors, depending primarily on how many there are of them, on whether there is a dominant leader, on whether market demand is growing, and on the overall supply-demand balance in the industry; other pressures come from barriers to exit, the existence of which can force players to stay and fight, rather than flee.

- *The threat of new entrants*—which is higher when barriers to entry, whether in capital, technology, operations or personnel, are lower, or when customer switching costs are low.

- *The existence of substitute products or solutions*—which customers could turn to or switch to, thereby abandoning your industry.

- *Supplier bargaining power*—often a reflection of the numbers of suppliers or the presence of one or two domi-

Figure 1.2 **The forces of industry competition**

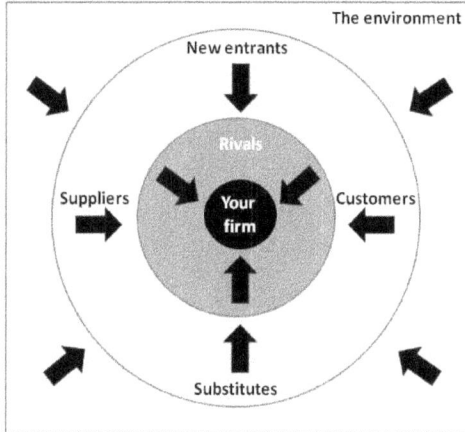

nant suppliers.

- *Customer bargaining power*—as with supplier power, often dependent on numbers or the extent of dominance by one or two customers.

- *Environmental factors*—such as Government subsidies, regulation, trade unions (where restrictive practices can raise barriers to entry) or industry/environment/employment law.

In some industries, such as soft drinks, software, toiletries, these pressures operate benignly to boost profitability—and consistently over the decades. In others, like airlines or textiles, the opposite is true—each of the pressures acts against the players and average profitability over the years is poor.

How tough are each of these pressures in your industry? High, low, medium? Or somewhere in between?

Combine all the pressures and how intense is overall competition in your industry?

Blockbusted

Blockbuster stores were ubiquitous in the early 2000s. From a single store in Dallas in 1985, the company had grown to 9,000, employing 60,000 people and with a market cap peaking at $5 billion.

Blockbuster had weathered triumphantly most of the industry pressures it faced:

- *Internal rivalry*—it has seen off or acquired most rivals over the years including its largest competitor, Hollywood Video.

- *The threat of new entrants*—greatly diminished, due to its dominance of the industry.

- *The presence of substitute products or solutions*— see below.

- *Environmental factors*— no significant pressures.

- *Supplier bargaining power*—its dominance enabled it to dictate terms to movie and game suppliers.

- *Customer bargaining power*—customers had the option of mom-and-pop stores or smaller chains, but these didn't carry the volumes or range of a Blockbuster store; customers stayed loyal despite somewhat punitive late return fees.

In 2000 Blockbuster had the opportunity to acquire for $50m a startup online DVD subscription postal operator with a nascent streaming service. It opted instead to develop its own offering, albeit four years behind. Netflix now has a market cap of $40 billion.

One industry pressure alone had been sufficient to scupper Blockbuster—the substitute solution. The alternative offering of Netflix, also of Hulu, proved such a disruptor that the blocks and mortar movie rental store was busted.

Repeat the exercise for each of your main segments. How does competitive intensity differ in each segment?

And what of the future? Is industry competition set to intensify? Because however tough it is at the moment, it results in you and your competitors getting an average operating margin of a certain percent.

But may competitive forces conspire to threaten that margin over the next few years?

If so, you will need to factor that into your KISSTRATEGY development of Chapter 2.

Identifying customer buying criteria

"All business success rests on something labeled a sale, which at least momentarily weds company and customer", wrote Tom Peters.

But why does that customer buy from that company? That is the question.

What do customers in one of your main segments need from you and your competitors? Are they looking for the lowest possible price for a given level of product (or service)? The highest quality product irrespective of price? Or something in between?

Do customers have the same needs in your other business segments? Do some customer groups place greater importance on certain needs?

What exactly do they want in terms of product? The highest specifications? Fastest delivery? The most reliable? The best technical back-up? The most sympathetic customer service?

Customer needs from their suppliers are called customer buying criteria and can usefully be grouped into six categories (see Figure 1.3). They are customer needs relating to the:

• *Effectiveness* of the product (or service) in terms, for example, of quality, design, features, specifications, functionality, reliability.

- *Efficiency* of the service, getting it to the customer conveniently and on time.

- *Range* of products (or services) provided.

- *Relationship* with the producer.

- *Premises* (only applicable if the customer needs to visit the supplier's premises).

- *Price*, which tends to be a more important criterion the less essential the product (or service).

They can be conveniently remembered, with perhaps droid-like undertones, as the E2-R2-P2 of customer buying criteria.

Which of these criteria are most important to your customers? How does importance differ in each of your main segments? Are any likely to become more or less important over time?

Once you have identified these customer buying criteria, and

Figure 1.3 **The E2-P2-R2 of customer buying criteria**

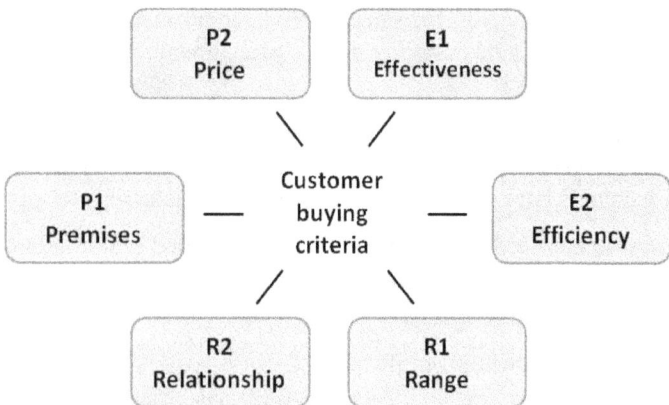

44

> **KISS tip**
>
> All this is very well in theory, you may ask, but how do you know what customers want? Simple. Ask them!
>
> It doesn't take long. You'd be surprised how after just a few discussions with customers from any one group a predictable pattern begins to emerge. Some may consider one need 'very important', others just 'important'.
>
> But it's unlikely that another will say that it's 'unimportant'. Customers in any one group tend to have similar needs.

their relative levels of importance, you will be able move on to the next challenge—what your firm and your competitors need to do to successfully meet these criteria.

Deriving factors for success

What do firms in your industry need to do to succeed? What factors are key to success?

What do you need to get right to satisfy customer buying criteria *and* run a sound business?

Such factors may be product (or service) quality, consistency, availability, range, and product development (R&D). On the service side, factors can include distribution capability, sales and marketing effectiveness, customer service, and post-sale technical support.

Other factors relate to the cost side of things, such as location of premises, scale of operations, state-of-the-art, cost effective equipment, and operational process efficiency.

To identify which are the most important factors for success in each of your main business segments, you need to undertake these steps:

- Identifying factors needed to meet buying criteria.

- Assessing management and market share.

- Rating these factors for importance.

- Identifying any must-haves.

Let's look briefly at each of these steps.

Identifying factors needed to meet buying criteria

Here you convert the customer buying criteria you identified above into factors for success. In other words, you work out *what your business has to do to meet your customer's needs*.

These factors can often be the flipside to customer buying criteria. The customer may seek functionality, so research and development will be a factor for success. The customer may seek product reliability, so quality control will be a factor for success. Delivery to schedule may be a customer buying criterion, so spare capacity and/or manufacturing efficiency may be a factor for success. These are factors in which you can differentiate your product or service from the competition—known rather ungainly as differentiation-related success factors.

There's one customer buying criterion that needs special attention, and that's price. Customers of most services expect a keen *price*. Producers need to keep their *costs* down. Price is a customer buying criterion, cost competitiveness a factor for success.

Determinants of cost competitiveness in your business could include location of facilities, cost of materials, operational efficiency, use of subcontractors, outsourcing of business processes, overhead control, remuneration levels, IT systems. These are cost-related success factors.

And size may be important. Other things being equal, the larger the business the lower costs should be *for each unit* of business sold. These are 'economies of scale' and may apply

> **KISS tip**
>
> Don't end up with too many factors for success or you
> may lose the wood for the trees. Market share, man-
> agement, two or three cost-related factors and five or
> six differentiation-related factors should be fine—a
> total of 10 or so.

not just to the unit cost of materials or other variable costs,
where a larger business will benefit from negotiated volume
discounts, but also to overheads, such as marketing, where the
same expense on, for example, a magazine advertisement or a
trade show stand can be spread over a larger volume base.

Assessing management and market share

We have derived two sets of factors from the customer buying
criteria set out above: differentiation-related and cost-related.
There are two more specific factors to be considered: management and market share.

How important is management in general in your industry?
Think on whether a well managed company, with a superb
sales and marketing team reinforced by an efficient operations
team, but with an average product, would outperform a poorly
managed company with a superb product in your industry.

There's one final factor—an important one—that we need to
take into account that isn't directly derived from customer
buying criteria: market share. The larger the market share, the
stronger typically the provider.

A high market share can manifest itself in a number of different competitive advantages. One such area is in lower unit
costs, but we've already covered this under economies of
scale, so we must be careful not to double count.

Market share is an indicator of the breadth and depth of your
customer relationships and your business reputation. Since it
is more difficult to gain a new customer than to do repeat business with an existing customer, the provider with the larger
market share typically has a competitive advantage—*the*

power of the incumbent.

The power of the incumbent rises in proportion to the switching costs—not just the financial costs of switching, but the time, hassle and even emotional costs. It's less of a wrench to change your printer than your accountant.

Rating these factors for importance

You've set out which are the most important factors for success in your business. But just how important are they, one with another? Run through each one and assign a rating: is it of high importance, medium or low? Or somewhere in between?

You may prefer, like me, to use a simple quantitative approach. You can give a weight, to the nearest 5 or 10%, as to the relative importance of each factor and juggle around with the weights until you have a realistic allocation which, crucially, tots up to 100%.

The great advantage of a quantitative approach is that you'll be able to deploy a simple Excel chart in Chapter 2 to derive a rating of the overall competitive position of your business. This can then be compared with ratings over time and with those of your competitors.

But, in the interests of KISS, and appreciating that not every reader feels comfortable with a quantitative approach, rest assured that rating factors in words such as of high or low importance can work just as well.

Figure 1.4 shows an example of the factors for success identified in a niche engineering market which I worked on a few years ago. The factors are rated for importance in words (column 2) and then in numbers (column 3). The choice is yours…!

Identifying any must-haves

There is one final wrinkle. But it may be crucial.

Is one of the success factors in your business so important that

Figure 1.4 Factors for success: an example

Factors for success in engineering niche market	Importance	Weight
Market share	Med/high	15%
Cost factors	Very high	35%
Differentiation factors:		
Product capability and range	Med/high	15%
Product reliability	Med/high	15%
Engineering service network	Med	10%
Customer service	Med	10%
Total weighting		**100%**

if you don't rank highly against it you shouldn't even be in business? You simply won't begin to compete, let alone succeed? You won't win any business, or you won't be able to deliver on the business you win? In other words, it is a *must-have* factor, rather than a mere *should-have*.

Must a business in your marketplace have, for example, the right ISO classification to win future orders in a competitively intensifying environment? Must a provider of your service have a specific degree or qualification before being able to attract a single customer?

Are any of the factors for success in your industry must-haves? You'll need to bear this in mind when assessing your firm's competitive position in Chapter 2.

Acknowledging competition in a startup

Too many startup business plans are based on the premise that theirs is a new, revolutionary concept. Competition is non-existent, or irrelevant.

In the vast majority of cases, this presumption is both wrong and dangerous. At best it is only ever only partially true.

There is always competition. Whatever is your solution to the perceived needs of the customer, someone else somewhere else has another solution.

Or will have. If they don't have a solution now, they may well have once they have seen yours.

So you need to look at three aspects of competition in a startup:

- Direct competition.
- Indirect competition.
- Competitive response.

Direct competition

If your new venture is a business with a clearly defined existing marketplace, then your analysis of industry competition will be no different from that of an established business.

You'll identify the competitors, soon to be augmented by one, and assess competitive intensity, soon to be intensified perhaps by your firm's entry.

An example, as introduced in the section on market demand, would be a startup boutique specializing in designer childrenswear on Main St. Your competitors would include: other such boutiques; any boutiques focusing on adult clothes but also offering a selection for children; childrenswear chain-stores; the childrenswear departments of department stores; and all of these variants using alternative routes to market, especially via online or catalogue shopping.

You will be entering a highly competitive market—retail can

KISS tip

If your firm fares well, it will ring a bell—for the competitor as for the customer.

---

be an unforgivingly competitive arena—but hopefully with a distinctive edge that you will set out forcefully in Chapter 2.

Indirect competition

What if your idea is a genuinely new concept? Who are your competitors?

They are whoever was providing an alternative solution to the customer before your business existed, competing for a similar share of the customer's wallet as you are.

Suppose you invented an ingenious wooden roller-ball back massaging device which released aromatherapy oils as you massaged. It's new, it's unique, it's brilliant, it works!

But it has competition. The customer's need is relief from back tension or discomfort. The customer is prepared to dip into her pocket to relieve that pain.

She has a range of alternative solutions—other wooden roller-ball devices, plastic and metal versions, electrically powered massage devices, massage chairs. She can go to a masseur, even an aromatherapist. She can purchase the oils and self-administer. She can take pills.

All these are competitors, even if only indirect ones. Yours will occupy a particular price positioning—above basic roller-ball devices, below power-driven ones—but the customer has the option to trade up or down.

In the next chapter, you'll consider the pros and cons of alternative solutions. You'll lay out your stall. But it's a stall in relation to the alternative providers—and these competitors need to be identified in this chapter and the intensity of this competition assessed.

Competitive response

What will be the reaction of competitors, direct and indirect, if your venture turns out to be a success?

You cannot assume that they will stand idly by and cheer you on.

If your new concept is patent protected, that is great. But could there be ways for a nimble competitor to negotiate a path around the patent, and legally? Offering a slight variant on the theme can often be enough.

And how will you respond not if but when your competitors respond to your market entry?

Suppose your childrenswear boutique is successful. How will the department store down the road respond? Perhaps by cordoning off the childrenswear department, refitting it with a whacky, kiddie-enthralling décor—or even engaging a clown every Saturday morning? How would you respond to that response?

Suppose your oil-infused roller-ball massaging device was successful? How will producers of basic devices respond? Will they copy the device if it is unpatented? If patented, could they offer their devices along with free-standing oils for self-administering at 15% below your price? How would you respond to that?

Consider competitive response. And prepare your retaliatory response to that response.

To summarize the main points of this chapter, you will by now have confirmed, let's hope, that your firm is operating in a market where, in its main segments,:

• Market demand is sizeable and growing.

• Industry competition is manageable.

• Demand will continue to exceed supply.

Next we look at your firm—how it is positioned in this market and how it can develop a sustainable competitive advantage.

2 Creating competitive advantage

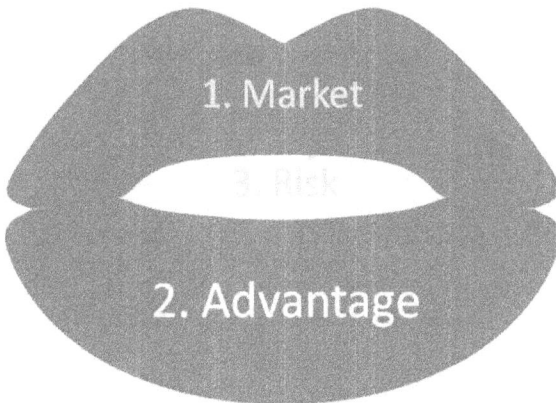

KISSTRATEGY

1. Market

3. Risk

2. Advantage

\\

If you don't have a competitive advantage, don't compete, Jack Welsh

In this chapter

- Tracking your competitive position
- Targeting the strategic gap
- Bridging the gap

In Chapter 1 you built the foundations for strategy development. You understand the market and where it is heading. Now you need to place your firm within that context.

You need to track its competitive position over time and pinpoint its competitive advantage. Then you should raise your sights. Figure out what the strategic gap is between the capabilities of your business now and those of the ideal player, now and in the future.

Finally, you look at ways in which you can bridge that gap. That is how you are going to create a sustainable competitive advantage for your firm.

We start with tracking competitive position.

Tracking your competitive position

You need to set out your firm's competitive position and pinpoint your competitive advantage—for each main business segment. And then do likewise for your main competitors.

This applies whether yours is an established business or a startup.

Competitive position in an established business

In Chapter 1 you identified what would be the key factors needed for success in your main business segments over the next few years. And you rated each by level of importance—or, if you were mathematically inclined, with an indicative percentage weighting.

How does you firm rate against each of those success factors?

How do your principal competitors rate?

What is your overall competitive position in each main segment? And theirs? How do your relative positions differ by segment?

You need to assess your competitive position, and that of each principal competitor, over time and for each main segment.

You could do this right now, at your desk, based on feedback you and your sales and purchasing teams have received from customers and suppliers over the years. Or you could do it more methodically, via a structured interviewing program with customers, ex-customers, potential customers, suppliers, and other industry observers.

You will assess your strengths and weaknesses and those of your peers. The process will pinpoint your sources of competitive advantage—as well as those of your most formidable competitors.

The process of deriving competitive position is straightforward: a 0-5 rating system works best. If your business performs about the same as your peers against a success factor, give it a score in the middle, a 3. If it performs very strongly, even dominantly, give it a 5. Poorly, a 1. If it performs not quite as well as most others, give it a 2. Better than most, a 4.

Now do the same for each of your principal competitors against that success factor. Who's the best performer against this factor? Does the company merit a 5, or are they better but not *that* much better than others, for a 4?

And so on against each success factor.

Arrange the information in a table:

- Success factors in column 1.

- Level of importance in column 2, in either words or symbols (if you are using MS Word) or indicative percentage weighting (if MS Excel).

- Your firm's rating in column 3.

- The ratings of each main competitor in columns 4 and 5, or more.

If you've used Excel, your competitive position will fall out at the bottom of the spreadsheet. If you prefer to stay in Word, you'll need to eyeball the ratings alongside the relative importance of each success factor and form your overall conclusion. You won't be far out.

Figure 2.1 gives an example in Word, taken from a recent strategy assignment. It shows that the company was the leading player in its niche engineering market, with a competitive position significantly above those of its two main competitors. But there was no room for complacency. Though the company had the largest presence in the market, the best engineering service network and a strong cost base, competitor A had developed a product with enhanced features and functionality that was proving attractive to customers. Competitor B, meanwhile, had a competitive cost base, but was still some way behind in both product and service capabilities.

Overall the company had the strongest competitive position, with a rating of roughly 4+, compared with its two main rivals' ratings of 3.5+ and 3+. Note that these overall ratings were derived from eyeballing ratings against each factor against the relative importance of the factor—not a scientific approach, but one that is very much preferable to using no weighting at all.

Better though to use indicative percentage weightings for each success factor and leave it to Excel to derive the exact competitive position. Using the percentage weightings of Figure 1.3, the company's competitive position emerged as 4.2, com-

Figure 2.1 Competitive position: an example

Factors for success in engineering niche market	Importance	The company	Competitor A	Competitor B
Market share	Med/high	5	3.5	2
Cost factors	Very high	4	3.5	4.5
Differentiation factors:				
Product capability and range	Med/high	4	4.5	3
Product reliability	Med/high	4	4	2.5
Engineering service network	Med	5	3.5	2.5
Customer service	Med	3	3	2
Overall competitive position		4+	3.5+	3+

Key: 1 = Weak, 2 = Tenable, 3 = Favorable, 4 = Strong, 5 = Dominant

pared to its main rival's 3.7.

Competing by segment

Apply the same process for each of your main segments. You'll find that your competitive position will likely differ from segment to segment. This may be because one success factor in which you are particularly strong (or weak) has a lesser importance in one segment than another.

Or it may be that you are simply stronger in one segment than another. For instance, your business may have an enviable track record in service and repair in one segment, but you haven't long been in another—rating a 5 in the first, but only a 2 in the other.

Competing over time

So far your analysis of competitive position has been static.

You've rated your firm's current competitiveness and those of others. But that's only the first part of the story. How has your competitive position changed over the last few years and how is it likely to change over the next few years? You need to understand the dynamics. Is it set to improve or worsen?

The simplest way to do this is to add an extra column to your chart, representing your position in, say, three years' time. Then you can build in any improvements in your ratings against each success factor. These prospective improvements need, for the time being, to be both in the pipeline *and* likely. In the next section we shall assess how you can *proactively and systematically* improve your competitive position. That's strategy. But for now it is useful to see how your competitive position seems set to evolve naturally over the next few years, assuming no significant change in strategy.

Remember, however, that improved competitive position is a two-edged sword. Your competitors too will have plans. This is where the analysis gets challenging. You know what you're planning to do but what are your competitors up to?

Try adding a couple of further columns representing your two most fearsome competitors as they may be in three years' time. Do you have any idea what they're planning to do to improve their competitiveness in the near future? What are they likely to do? What could they do? *What are you afraid they'll do?*

Returning to the example of the UK niche engineering company, management was aware that competitor A had plans to outsource certain components to reduce cost and to set up a joint venture to enhance its engineering service capability. A's strategy seemed set to narrow the competitive gap unless the company deployed a proactive strategy focused on research and development—see Figure 2.2.

Getting past first base

In the last section, we introduced the concept of the must-have success factor—without a good rating in which your business cannot even begin to compete.

Figure 2.2   **Future competitive position: an example**

Factors for success in engineering niche market	Importance	The company	Competitor A	Competitor A tomorrow
Market share	Med/High	5	3.5	4
Cost factors	Very high	4	3.5	4
Differentiation factors:				
Product capability and range	Med/High	4	4.5	4.5
Product reliability	Med/High	4	4	4
Engineering service network	Med	5	3.5	4
Customer service	Med	3	3	3.5
Overall competitive position		4+	3.5+	4

Key: 1 = Weak, 2 = Tenable, 3 = Favorable, 4 = Strong, 5 = Dominant

Did you find a must-have factor in any of your business segments? If so, how do you rate against it? Strong or favorable? Fine. Tenable? Questionable. Weak? Troublesome. A straight zero, not even a 1? You're out. You don't get past first base.

And what about in a few years' time? Could any factor develop into a must-have? How will you rate then? Will you get past first base?

And even though you rate as tenable against a must-have factor today, might it slip over time? Could it slide below 2, into tricky territory?

This may be a case of being cruel to be kind. It's better to know. The sooner you realize that you're in a wrong segment, the sooner you can withdraw and focus resources on the right segments.

Implications for future market share

This competitive position analysis plays a useful role in business planning. It gives you an idea of how your firm is likely to fare over the next few years *in relation to the market as a whole.*

If your overall competitive position turns out to be around 3, or good/favorable, you should, other things being equal, be able to grow business *in line with the market* over the next few years. In other words, to hold market share.

If it is around 4 or above, you should be able to *beat the market,* to gain market share, again, other things being equal. Suppose you forecast market demand growth of 10 percent a year in Chapter 1. With a strong competitive position, rated at around 4, you should feel comfortable that you can grow your business at, say, 12-15 percent a year.

If your competitive position is around 2, however, you'll be less confident about your business prospects. It's more likely you'll *underperform the market* and if your boss is expecting the firm to outpace the market something will have to change!

Implications for strategy development

Competitive position analysis also throws up some facts and judgments highly useful for strategy development:

- How you compete overall in key segments—hence where you are most likely to be most profitable relative to the competition.

- Areas of strength in key segments, which can be built on.

- Areas of weakness in some segments, which may need to be worked on.

- Areas of strength or weakness common to many or all segments, which could well be a priority to build or work on.

- Relative competitiveness in each key segment.

- Change in competitiveness over time.

- In summary, your source of competitive advantage,

tracked over time.

It will form the basis for identification of the strategic gap in the next section.

Competitive position for a startup

The process set out in this section is not that different for a startup, whether serving an existing market or creating a new one. You need to assess your likely competitive position in the main segments where you intend to compete and develop a strategy to enhance that competitiveness over time.

There are three main differences:

- Your competitive position is in the future tense rather than the present tense.

- It will be affected adversely from the outset by a low rating against all key success factors pertaining to experience.

- You must nevertheless have some evident competitive advantage just to survive in the early years.

Your competitive position in a new venture is a judgment more on the immediate future than the present. For an estab-

---

KISS tip

Too much analysis hinders decision-making—don't do this competitive position analysis for too many segments, too many success factors, too many competitors or too many years, past and future. KISS—opt for the main segments, the main success factors, the main competitors, now and three years' hence; look for the main findings, the key lessons; drill down further only if necessary and potentially illuminating.

Not just a hill of beans

Imagine eating a chocolate bar and knowing exactly which farm in which country the cocoa beans which make it come from—then being able to compare it to other chocolate bars with cocoa from a different farm or different country, each with a subtly distinctive flavor. At a price, of course.

That is what the consumer can get with so-called bean-to-bar chocolate. And that must have been a terrific niche for the original such chocolatier, but, alas, as has happened likewise with craft beers and spirits, other producers piled in and there are now dozens of bean-to-bar chocolatiers in the US and Europe.

What is distinctive about one of them is the pains he has gone to transform his suppliers into partners. Former lawyer Shawn Askinosie ploughs 10% of profits from Missouri-based Askinosie Chocolate back to his farmer suppliers in Ecuador, Tanzania, Honduras, and the Philippines.

He has created a distinctive offering less through the product itself than the benefit it conveys to the consumer, namely the satisfaction conveyed of ethical sourcing and supplier empowerment. The typical customer seems prepared to pay a higher price for a specifically sourced chocolate bar and may be prepared to pay just a little bit extra again in the knowledge that a share of the profits will return to the cocoa farmer.

It is a clever competitive advantage, and one which also serves to motivate employees, let alone suppliers and customers, but is unlikely to be sustainable. If it works, and Askinosie Chocolate is already turning over $2 million, it will be copied. But in the meantime, in the words of Schultz, apropos The Beatles: *'All you need is love— but a little chocolate now and then doesn't hurt'.*

lished business, the debate revolves as much around the present and recent past as it does the future—around the weighting of success factors and/or your ratings against them, as justified by evidence from customer, supplier, and other interviews, each of which will be as much based on fact and performance track record as judgment.

But for a startup, the debate will be part conjecture, especially if your venture is to a new market. There is no track record of your performance, nor maybe on the market. For the latter, though, you must find evidence from any which source—see Chapter 1.

There is nothing you can do about your new venture's rating against those success factors which demand experience. Thus your rating against market share will be low at the outset, so too perhaps against some cost-related factors, especially those relating to scale.

Likewise your rating against some differentiation factors may be low. Your lack of track record may count against you in consistency of product quality, delivery, customer service or sales and marketing.

In that case, how will your firm compete? The answer is that it's not easy being a new entrant in an existing market. Your competitive position will indeed be low relative to the leaders at the outset. But if you are addressing a growing market and/ or you can differentiate your product or service sufficiently, things should improve. Your competitive position in three to five years time should have improved measurably—your market share rating should be up, your unit costs down, your service performance improved.

But this analysis further highlights the importance of segmentation. If your new venture does not serve an existing market but creates its own, then all changes. The analysis of competition will be undertaken not for the market as a whole but for your addressed product/market segment. And if that is a new segment, created by your new venture, you effectively have no direct competition.

But there are two caveats:

- You will have indirect competition, as discussed in Chapter 1, who may up their game if you are successful.

- You will in time face competition from new entrants, if your new market is worthy of pursuit.

To survive the hostile early years of a startup, you must create a distinct competitive advantage. This can take a multitude of forms, including most commonly:

- A new product (or service).

- A similar product but at lower cost.

- A similar product but with a distinct element of differentiation, whether in quality (features, functionality, reliability?), distribution (electronic rather than physical?), delivery, service (pre-sale help, after-sale care?), marketing (a theme which resonates?).

- A similar product tailored to a new market.

- A similar product offered to a new region.

Whatever your source of perceived competitive advantage, it must carry enough weight to give your new business at least a tenable competitive position in those early years of the venture.

If your venture manages no more than a rating of 1 (out of 5) for market share, as is likely, 1.5 for cost factors, also likely in the early days, 2 for product quality, 2 for service and 2 for delivery, that will give you a startup competitive position below 2, depending on success factor weightings.

Of dames and detectives

We saw above how Askinosie Chocolate identified a competitive advantage.

What real life examples spring to your mind? Think of a company you admire. What is its source of competitive advantage? Is it sustainable?

I always enjoy reading of a small company that has made it. By making it, I am not talking about some stellar entrepreneur doing an Apple or a Facebook. But an entrepreneur surviving and earning enough for a comfortable lifestyle for the family.

The vast majority of businesses are small and it always saddens me to hear of one going under. Each founder has shown such spirit, such initiative, such courage to set out on his or her own that few merit such a fate.

But often the failure of a small business comes about because it does not possess a sustainable competitive advantage. It is, in effect, a me-too business.

Here is my personal favorite example of a business with a sustainable competitive advantage—fictional, but no less educational for that.

The No 1 Ladies Detective Agency was launched by Alexander McCall Smith's wonderfully warm, wise, and witty creation, Mma Precious Ramotswe, in downtown Gaborone, the capital of Botswana. She captures business through being the first and only female detective agency in town—an initial source of differentiation and competitive advantage. And it is a sustainable advantage—even if a direct competitor were to emerge, Mma Ramotse's would remain undeniably, and forever, the first, hence No 1, ladies detective agency!

What is your firm's competitive advantage? Is it sustainable?

That is untenable. Your startup has no distinct competitive advantage. It will fail.

If, however, you manage to earn a rating of 4, even 5, against a couple of those success factors, in those specific areas of your competitive advantage, your initial competitive position may emerge closer to 2.5 or 3—which is not too bad for a startup, given the inevitably low ratings against market share, cost factors and management in the early days. It is a tenable, bordering on favorable, competitive position.

The key to a successful startup, to repeat, is competitive advantage, somehow, in some form, but distinct.

For further reading on competitive advantage in a startup, try John Mullins' terrific book, *The New Business Road Test*. This is essential reading on the preparatory work and research you should undertake before firming up a strategy for a startup, especially in a new market.

Targeting the strategic gap

"We know what we are, but know not what we may be", William Shakespeare

You have worked out the current competitive position of your business. Where do you want it to be in three to five years' time? What is your target competitive position?

You need to identify the gap between where you are now and where the ideal player is, now and in the future. You will then set your sights on the extent to which you aim to narrow, even bridge that gap.

There are two distinct types of gap:

- In which segments you should compete—the portfolio gap.

- How well you compete in each segment—the capability gap.

The portfolio and capability gaps together form the strategic gap. Here you will identify and target the gap. In the next section you will look at the strategic options for bridging it.

The portfolio gap

Where should your business compete? In which segments? How can you enhance the strategic position of your business?

What should your portfolio of business segments look like? What s the gap from today's portfolio?

Note that this section may be less relevant in a startup, where the focus can often be on one segment only, at least in the early stages. If that is the case with your business, please proceed to the next section on the capability gap.

The attractiveness/advantage matrix, an invaluable business tool, portrays the strategic position of your business portfolio. It shows how competitive your business is in each segment, ranked in terms of market attractiveness. You should invest ideally in segments where you are strongest and/or which are the most attractive. And you should consider withdrawal from segments where you are weaker and/or where your competitive position is untenable.

And perhaps you should be looking to enter another business segment (or segments) in more attractive markets than the ones you currently address? If so, do you have grounds for believing that you would be at least reasonably placed in this new segment? And that you soon could become well placed?

First, you need to specify how to define an 'attractive' market segment. This is to some extent sector-specific, but over the years I have found these five factors to be both pertinent and relatively measurable in most sectors:

- Market size.
- Market demand growth.
- Competitive intensity.
- Industry profitability.

- Market risk—cyclicality, volatility (for example, exposure to country risk).

The larger the market and the faster it is growing, the more attractive, other things being equal, is the market. Likewise the greater the industry profitability. But be careful with the other two factors, where the converse applies. The *greater* the competitive intensity and the *greater* the risk, the *less* attractive is the market.

An example may help (see Figure 2.3). Suppose your business is in four segments and you are contemplating entering a fifth. You rate each of the segments against each of the criteria for market attractiveness. For the sake of KISS, you take a simple average to arrive at a measure of overall attractiveness. Segment D emerges as the most attractive, followed by new segment E. B is rather unattractive.

Next you pull out the ratings of competitive position you undertook in the last section (for example Figure 2.1), for each

Figure 2.3 **Market attractiveness: an example**

Segments:	A	B	C	D	E (new)
Market size	3	2	2	3	3
Market growth	1	2	3	5	5
Competitive Intensity	2	2	3	4	5
Industry profitability	3	3	4	2	2
Market risk	5	2	4	4	2
Overall attractiveness	2.8	2.2	3.2	3.6	3.4

Key to rating: 1 = Unattractive, 3 = Reasonably Attractive, 5 = Highly Attractive
[For competitive intensity, remember that the more intense the competition, the *less* attractive the market. Likewise for market risk: the riskier the market, the *less* attractive]

Figure 2.4   **Strategic position: an example**

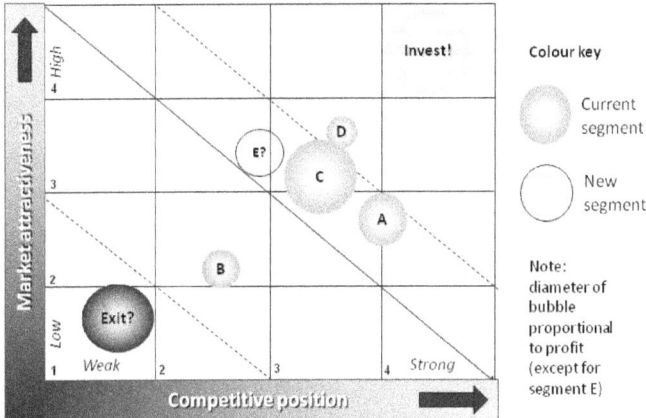

Source: General Electric, McKinsey & Co., and various

segment. Now you can draw up the attractiveness/advantage chart, by placing each segment in the appropriate part of the matrix (see Figure 2.4). Segment A, for example, has a competitive position rating of 4 (out of 5) and a market attractiveness rating of 2.8 (also out of 5).

The segment's position in the chart will reflect both its competitive position (along the x-axis) and its market attractiveness (along the y-axis). The size of each circle should be roughly proportional to the segment's contribution to operating profit.

The closer your segment is positioned towards the top right-hand corner the better placed it is. Above the top right dotted diagonal, you should invest further in that segment, building on your advantage. Should the segment sink below the bottom left dotted diagonal, however, you should harvest the business for cash or consider withdrawal. Segments placed along the main diagonal are reasonably placed and should be held, with investment cases carefully scrutinized.

The overall strategic position shown in the example seems

> **KISS tip**
>
> A major criticism of this portfolio planning tool lies in its subjectivity. Some argue that so many judgment calls are made throughout the process that deriving strategy from its findings is fraught with danger.
>
> But strategy is all about judgment, albeit backed up by fact where available. The very process of constructing the matrix, taking in work done earlier, is illuminating, instructive and crucial to strategy development. It forces you to think about what drives success in your business, how your business fares against those drivers and what you need to do to fare better in the future. It is not only a portfolio planning tool, but the first step in identifying the strategic gap.
>
> No strategy tools can obviate the need for judgment. Nor should they be expected to.

sound. It shows favorable strength in the biggest and reasonably attractive segment, C, and an excellent position in the somewhat less attractive segment A. Segment D is highly promising and demands more attention, given the currently low level of profit.

Segment B should perhaps be exited—it's a rather unattractive segment, and your firm is not that well placed. The new segment E seems promising.

You may consider the following strategic options worthy of further analysis :

- Holding and steady development in segments A and C.
- Investment in segment D.
- Entry to segment E (with competitive position improving over time as market share develops).
- Harvesting or exit from segment B.

How is the overall strategic position in your business? Hopefully your main segments, from which you derive most revenues, should find themselves positioned above the main diagonal.

Do you have any new segments in mind? How attractive are they? How well placed would you be?

Are there any segments you should be thinking of getting out of? Be careful here, though. Would withdrawal from one segment adversely affect your position in another? Might it be better to persevere with a loss leader?

Which segments are so important that you would derive greatest benefit from improving your competitive position? Where should you concentrate your efforts?

The capability gap

You have targeted the portfolio gap. Next up is the capability gap.

Targeting the capability gap can be undertaken in four stages:

- Envision future scenarios.
- Profile the ideal player.
- Stretch your sights.
- Specify the target gap.

Start with the crystal ball.

Envision future scenarios

Try envisioning the future of your marketplace. Will it be more competitive? Will customers have different expectations? Will players need to develop different capabilities?

Try thinking 'out of the box', using the imagination, stimulating the right side of the brain. Try brainstorming.

Try to develop a range of scenarios on what may happen in

your marketplace. Venture beyond the more likely outcomes—you've already drawn those up. Think of those that are less expected but still *quite* likely to occur. Stay clear of fanciful outcomes with only a remote chance of happening. Go for scenarios that could actually happen.

Under such scenarios, will customer needs and buying criteria change? Which success factors will become more prominent? Which less so?

Profile the ideal player

We can define the ideal player in your marketplace as the one who would achieve the highest possible rating against each of the success factors identified—whether those of today or those which you have identified as becoming more prominent in the future.

How close to becoming this ideal player should you aim?

Stretch your sights

What is the gap between your firm's capabilities now and those to which you aspire? Should you reconsider where you aim to be? Are you sure you've set sufficiently challenging goals?

Should you be stretching your sights?

Where do you want to be in tomorrow's marketplace? Do you want to become a good player in tomorrow's marketplace? A strong player?

Or do you want to *lead* in tomorrow's marketplace?

Do you want to get as far as you can toward becoming the Ideal Player of Tomorrow? Do you want to go for goal?—see Figure 2.5.

If so, remember that the goalposts may well have shifted by the time you're ready to shoot. Time moves on, and the ideal player in five years' time will have a different mix of capabilities to the equivalent today. Perhaps only with slight differ-

Figure 2.5　**Going for goal**

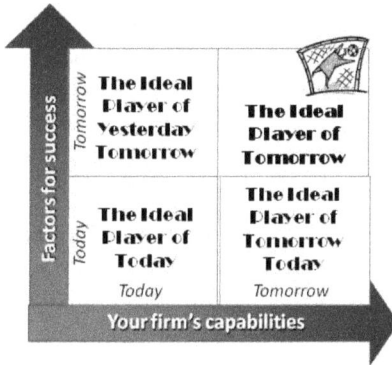

ences in nuance, perhaps radically different.

The *Going for Goal* chart highlights three important points:

- It's fine being the *Ideal Player of Today*, but today only lasts one day.

- If your firm doesn't develop the extra capabilities required to meet the customer needs of tomorrow, you'll become the *Ideal Player of Yesterday Tomorrow*.

- There's little point in developing extra capabilities today unless customers need them, or you'll become the *Ideal Player of Tomorrow Today*.

Once you've raised your sights, perhaps to the very top, you need to specify the capability gap and, in the next section, plan how you are going to bridge it.

Specify the capability gap

You need to revisit the competitive position charts you drew up at the start of Chapter 2. Check for any changes over time in the weighting of success factors as a result of changes in the external marketplace, given the scenario development you have undertaken above.

You can now identify the capability gap. Whatever rating you have given your business in three years' time, it is unlikely that you have arrived at a 5 against each success factor. Any shortfall below a 5 represents a capability gap with the ideal player.

But is it reasonable to believe you could achieve a 5 in each success factor over the next few years? Unlikely. Better to set yourself a realistic target, albeit one that is stretched and challenging. Against which factor should you be raising your game? And by how much?

You now target that gap. Often that means just the insertion of an active verb, such as 'improve'. You have found a capability gap in your distribution—targeting that gap means improving distribution.

Sometimes targeting the gap requires further thought. The capability gap may be too broad and you might consider exiting the segment.

Let's return to the example we used earlier in this chapter of the business operating in four main segments and contemplating entry to another. As a result of profiling the ideal player and raising sights, the CEO might now target the capability gap as follows:

- Improve margin in segment A.
- Withdraw in segment B, recognizing an unbridgeable gap.
- Improve distribution in segment C.
- Improve product speed to market in segment D.
- Enter segment E.
- Lower production costs across all segments.

Figure 2.6 **Strategic repositioning: an example**

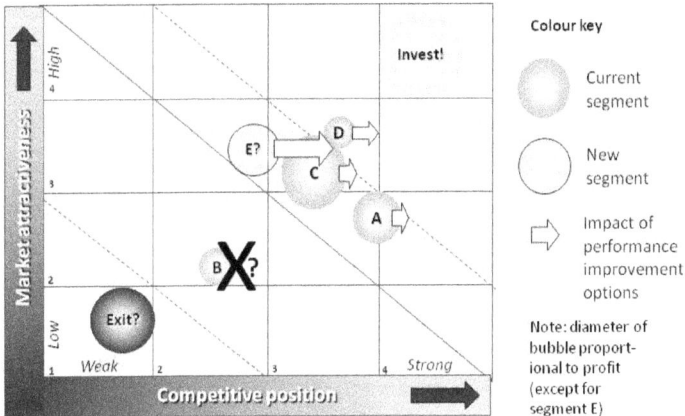

- Improve enterprise resource management ('ERM') systems across the business.

The impact of this targeting of the capability gap could be as shown in Figure 2.6. The competitive position of each segment, especially E, should be improved, other than B, which will be exited. The overall strategic position of this business could be greatly improved.

Note that targeting the capability gap does not at this stage specifying the means of how it will be achieved. That is left for the strategic options in the next section.

Improving distribution is an example of targeting a capability gap. Switching to a new distributor is a strategic option.

Lowering production costs across all segments is targeting a capability gap. Outsourcing or offshoring is a strategic option.

One happy Christmas

The capability gap was infinite when Mac Harman's brother-in-law sneezed—he was allergic to the Christmas tree. Mac offered to replace it with a top quality, identical artificial one, but couldn't find one—none such existed.

That gave Mac an idea. He travelled to China and soon had designs for highly realistic, if pricey, imitations of the likes of the Norway Spruce, the Nordmann Fir and the Silverado Slim. He imported 5,000 units in October 2006, set up a pop-up stall in Stanford, CA and a website and sold out well before Christmas.

Balsam Brands also now sells high quality wreaths, garlands and ornaments and turns over $90m, with operations extended to Europe and the Far East. Mac had spotted a product gap and filled it. His favorite carol: *"O Christmas tree, O Christmas tree, much pleasure thou canst give me"*?

Targeting the gap for a startup

We concluded above that the secret to a successful startup is to hit the ground running with an evident competitive advantage.

But how defensible is that advantage?

If your new venture succeeds, you will be targeted. Competitors will eye your newly carved space with envy. They will come after you. And soon.

Remember the definition we used for strategy: Strategy is how a company deploys its scarce resources to gain a sustainable advantage over the competition. The all important word for a startup is *sustainable*.

How will you protect yourself against the inevitable competitive response? There are a number of ways you can try and sustain your competitive advantage:

> **KISS tip**
>
> Strategic gap analysis has its critics. Capabilities, they say, are not as easily developed as resources. And rectifying weaknesses may be less value enhancing than building on strengths. These are perfectly valid points—but use gap analysis anyway, along with your judgment and common sense.

- Patent protection of key products.

- Sustained innovation, staying one step ahead in product development.

- Sustained process improvement, staying one step ahead in cost competitiveness and efficiency.

- Investment in branding, identifying in the mind of the customer the particular befit brought by your offering with its name.

- Investment, for business-to-business ventures, in customer relationships.

The process for determining your strategy to counteract competitive response, however, is the same as for an established business above.

In profiling the ideal player, you should include in your envisioning a scenario where there is a ferocious competitive response to your presence from the competitor, direct or indirect, you most fear.

In specifying the target gap, you must go for goal—becoming the ideal player in your chosen niche market.

You must identify the capability gap between where you will be at launch and where the ideal player will be three to five years hence.

That is the gap you will target. Nothing less will do. The vast majority of new businesses fail in the first five years. You either eat or be eaten. You have to go for it, go for goal.

In the next section we shall look at how your new venture will set out to bridge the capability gap and sustain its competitive advantage.

Bridging the gap

"Don't be afraid to take a big step. You can't cross a chasm in two short jumps", David Lloyd George

You have identified and targeted the strategic gap. Now you need to bridge it.

We'll examine this in five sections:

- Opting for a generic strategy.
- Strategic repositioning and shaping profit growth options.
- Grouping into strategic alternatives
- Making the strategic investment decision.
- Bridging the gap for a startup.

We start with the generic strategies.

Opting for a generic strategy

Three generic business strategies have been with us since the early 1980s and should still form the starting point in your strategy development.

They are strategies (see Figure 2.7) of:

- Cost leadership.
- Differentiation.
- Focus.

Figure 2.7 **Three generic strategies**

Your competitive advantage

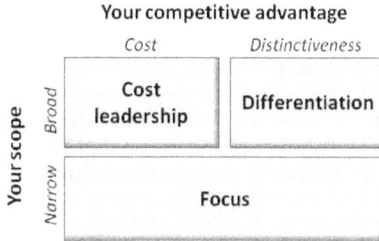

Source: Adapted from Michael E. Porter,
Competitive Strategy, Free Press, 1980

Any one of these strategies can yield sustainable competitive advantage. Pursue two or all three of these strategies in the same business and you will end up 'stuck in the middle'—a recipe for long-term under-performance.

What is the primary source of competitive advantage in your business? Is it cost? Or is it the distinctiveness of your product and/or service offering?

Think back to the start of this chapter where you rated your business against the factors for success in your industry. Did your business get higher ratings against the cost or the differentiation factors?

And go back one stage further. In Chapter 1 you identified and weighted these success factors in each key segment. Did you give a higher weighting to differentiation factors than to cost factors? Or the other way round?

There is little to be gained in being a cost leader in a segment which is not price sensitive. Likewise in being a highly differentiated producer in a segment where customers perceive little differentiation and demand only least cost.

If cost factors are most important in your business *and* you rated well or at least promisingly against them, then you should opt for a strategy of cost leadership.

If differentiating factors are more important *and* you rated well or at least promisingly against them, you should pursue a strategy of differentiation.

Either strategy can yield a sustainable competitive advantage. Either you supply a product (or service) that is at lower cost to competitors or you supply a product that is sufficiently differentiated from competitors that customers are prepared to pay a premium price for it—where the incremental price charged adequately covers the incremental costs of supplying the differentiated product.

For a ready example of a successful low cost strategy, think of SouthWest Airlines, where relentless maximization of load factor enables them to offer seats at scarcely credible prices compared with those that prevailed before they entered the scene. And they still make a profit. Or think of Ikea's stylish but highly price competitive furniture.

A classic example of the differentiation strategy is Apple: never the cheapest, whether in PCs, laptops, mobile phones or tablets, but always stylistically distinctive and feature-intensive.

Then there is the focus strategy. While acknowledging that a firm can typically prosper in its industry by following either a low-cost or differentiation strategy, one alternative is to not address the whole industry but narrow the scope and focus on a slice of it, a single segment.

Under these circumstances, a firm can achieve market leadership through focused differentiation leading over time to scale and experience-driven low unit costs compared to less focused players in that segment.

The classic example of a successful focus strategy is Honda motorcycles, whose focus on product reliability over decades yielded the global scale to enable its differentiated, quality

> **KISS tip**
>
> Go for one generic strategy or the other. Low cost or differentiation. Don't do what so many companies do and try for both. They end up stuck in the middle of the road and getting run over.

products to become and remain cost competitive.

While we are on motorcycles, look at Harley Davidson's turn-around strategy. On the verge of being wiped out by the likes of Honda, Kawasaki et al. in the 1970s, when some cruelly nicknamed it the Hardly Ableson, it opted to focus on the heavyweight segment and produce solid, throaty, cruiser bikes. This strategy pulled market share in the category back from under 20% to over 50%—and in the process created an iconic, 'Easy Rider'-style brand which has lasted to this day.

Be aware, though, that any generic strategy is vulnerable to shifting customer needs and preferences. No strategy should be set in stone.

If you pursue a low cost strategy, beware of a shift in customer needs putting a greater emphasis on quality, for which customers are prepared to pay a higher price. An example is the cinema industry. For years many chains followed a policy of shoving the customers into their 'flea pits', keeping costs down to a minimum. Customers deserted in droves, opting for the comfort of their living rooms and the ease of the video recorder. Today some cinemas offer reclining seats and waiter service—the diametrically opposite concept to the flea pit, and a service many customers will pay for.

Likewise, if you pursue a strategy of differentiation, beware of changing customer preferences. Customers may be prepared to shift to a new entrant offering a product or service of markedly inferior quality to yours, but good enough and at a significant price discount. The classic example is that of low cost airlines, originating in the U.S. and spreading rapidly to the U.K., Europe, and Asia, and forcing the full service national carriers to radically rethink their business model.

The canny business will spot the emergent trend and open a new business, preferably under a new brand, so as not to blur the image of the parent brand in the eyes of the customer. They will pursue one generic strategy in one business and a different one in another.

There is, however, no guarantee of success in the new business, given that it will operate in an entirely different culture—viz the attempts by Ford Motor Company to move into more differentiated businesses via acquisition: its Jaguar and Land Rover divisions soon had to be resold.

But it is especially inadvisable to mix strategies in one business, even if you are doing so in different segments. By definition, a strategic business unit operates in segments that are inter-related—whether by offering the same or similar products or services or addressing the same or similar customer groups. One strategy in one segment coupled with another strategy in another segment can not only confuse the customer but again land you 'stuck in the middle'.

Strategic repositioning and shaping profit growth options

You have set your generic strategy. What next?

You need to develop a series of profit growth options consistent with that strategy to bridge the strategic gap identified earlier in this chapter.

In targeting the portfolio gap you applied the Attractiveness/Advantage matrix to your business and concluded that you should invest in certain segments, hold in others and perhaps exit one or two—and, conversely, perhaps enter one or two new ones.

You also targeted the capability gap that needs to be bridged for your firm to achieve your target level of competitiveness in selected segments.

Now you will determine how to bridge the capability gap with profit growth options in each key segment to be invested in. Likewise for segments to be held—and perhaps even for those slated for exit. And you will consider the business as a whole and how it can be reshaped in line with your strategy to generate sustained profit growth.

Finally, you will differentiate between actions you can take now to increase profit in the short term (next 12 months) and those which will improve strategic position and grow profits in the long term.

Having drawn up a range of profit growth options you will evaluate them to decide which investment alternatives will yield the greatest return towards the goals and objectives of your firm.

Start by taking one segment at a time. Take those segments you have marked out for investing in, and then move on to those for holding, exit, and entry. Finally look at profit growth options which apply to all segments.

And always bear in mind the overall aim. Strategy is how a company deploys its scarce resources to gain a sustainable advantage over the competition. Here you are deciding in which segments and on which initiatives you should allocate those resources—to deliver that sustainable competitive advantage.

In *which* SEGMENTS and on *which* INITIATIVES should you allocate scarce resources to deliver **sustainable competitive advantage**?

Segments for investment

Take your largest segment, the one that gives the greatest contribution to overhead.

You have identified the capability gap in this segment. What are the options for bridging it?

The gap may be in new product speed to market. Bridging it may require streamlined processes. You may need to invest in expert advisers.

The gap may be in product reliability. Bridging it may require investment in new equipment, both in production and testing.

The gap may be in customer service. Bridging it may require investment in staff and training, even a cultural shift, achievable only through a controlled change management program.

In each of these examples, bridging the capability gap is a long-term process. That is often the case, but some profit growth options have faster results.

Indeed you should be on the look-out for short-term profit growth options. There is nothing like a quick win or two following a strategy development process to gladden the heart, justify the investment in time and energy and build team morale.

The quick win could come from a new angle in marketing, in its broadest sense—product, promotion, place, price— revealed in the strategy development process.

One such angle could be to lower prices. But that would reduce profit, not grow it, you might think. Perhaps, but maybe not for long:

- Volumes sold should increase, depending on the sensitivity (or technically 'price elasticity') of demand for the product, holding or growing revenue.

- Market share will be gained, enhancing your presence in the market and potentially stimulating further volume growth.

- Economies of scale may kick in, lowering your unit costs and restoring your operating margin (and even

Figure 2.8 **Strategic repositioning and performance improvement options**

Strategic repositioning options by segment	Performance improvement options	
	Short-term	Long-term
Invest	• Marketing • Lower pricing to gain share?	Bridge capability gap, invest in: • Fixed and current assets • Business processes • Staff & training
Hold	• Reduce variable cost • Tweak pricing?	• Reduce variable cost • Re-compete? • Alliance?
New	• Prepare project plan	• Leverage strengths
Exit	• Improve financials?	• Withdraw (sell?)
Whole business	• Benchmark overhead • Marketing	• Reduce overhead • BPR, outsourcing etc • Resource-based investment

gross margin, if your greater volumes enable you to drive down the unit costs of bought-in materials, components, and sub-assemblies).

These are some of the profit growth options, both short and long term, for bridging the capability gap in segments you will invest in. They are summarized in Figure 2.8.

Next you consider the profit growth options for those segments which you have chosen for holding—probably not to invest in, but definitely not to withdraw from.

Segments for holding

Holding on in a segment does not mean doing nothing, taking no strategic action. You need to actively manage your segment position and preferably strengthen it.

In the long term there are three profit growth options you should consider:

- Reduce variable cost—if you stand still on cost, you run the risk of a competitor under-cutting you over time; an ongoing program of cost reduction would be wise, whether in purchasing or operational efficiency.

- Re-compete—change the rules of the game in some way, so that you effectively create a new segment out of the old; look for inspiration to the iPhone, so much more than a mobile phone.

- Alliance—you have a favorable competitive position in a segment which is moderately attractive; perhaps by allying with a competitor you could jointly have a stronger position in that segment and enable superior profit growth prospects for both parties.

In the short term there are other options for you to consider. Cost reduction is both a short and long term option, but you may also consider tweaking your pricing in the segment, whether up or down:

- Nudging pricing up may change customer perceptions and give the impression that you are a premium player, though again you should think carefully on the price elasticity of demand; there are many examples of this strategy, such as the plethora of 'premium' beer brands exported to the US, in reality mass market beers in their home countries of Mexico, Netherlands, Belgium, Jamaica and others.

- Nudging pricing down, again depending on price elasticity, may gain you some extra volume and share, but beware of competitive retaliation.

Segments for exit

Profit growth options in those segments you have chosen to exit is limited. In corporate strategy, exiting a business unit can generate value through a structured sale process, including preparing the business for sale ('dressing the bride') and improving the financials pre-sale. In business strategy, your

---

KISS tip

Take care with the drawing up of profit growth options. The list should not get out of control.

Each option should satisfy two fundamental criteria:

- It should be consistent with your strategy.

- It should seem like a sound investment in itself.

Grouping the options into strategic alternatives further helps manage the process.

---

firm's presence in the business segments you choose to exit may have no sale value.

But there may be elements of value in that segment that can find a buyer. There may be some physical assets to sell or even some intangibles such as use of the brand name in that segment.

Segments for entry

You may have identified new segments your firm should consider entering. These should be segments where you can leverage your existing strengths.

A new product/market segment should be synergistic with your existing business, having one or more of these characteristics

- It is a new product (or service) related to your existing product range and sold to the same customer group.

- It is the same product but sold to a related customer group.

- [Remember that if it is both a new product *and* is being sold to a new customer group, that greatly amplifies risk and would require a much tougher degree of substantiation.]

- It is a segment where key success factors, both in cost and differentiation, mirror the relative strengths of your business.

- It is one in which some of your direct competitors are prospering and so might you.

- It is one in which some players in your line of business in other regions or countries are prospering and there seems no reason why the same should not apply in your region or country.

In the short term, you need to prepare a robust project plan for new segment entry and improve the odds on securing long term profit growth.

All segments

Finally you need to consider profit growth options that apply across all segments in your business.

Long term options may include:

- Reducing overhead costs, having benchmarked them against your competitors.

- Improving key business processes, perhaps through re-designing them.

- Outsourcing, perhaps even offshoring, business processes such as IT, technical support, customer services.

- Investing in the core competences of your business, whether they be in R&D, operations or sales.

- Marketing—leveraging the name of your business across all segments, which is also a potential profit growth option in the short term.

ENTerprising

Are your child's pesky tonsils playing up? Has your doctor recommended they come out? How about taking your kid to an organization that specializes in doing just that? Oh, and by the way, charges about one third below the national average?

Meet ENT Institute, a medical organization operating out of 15 locations around Atlanta, Georgia that does what it says in the name—it specializes in the treatment of ear, nose, and throat complaints. Period.

If your child is suffering from pimples, don't go there. If his or her knee gets twisted on the soccer field, go elsewhere. But if it's to do with the E, N or T, take a look at the website, where a full menu of treatments and charges is displayed transparently.

This is a classic if small scale example of the focus strategy. ENTI's offering is not only highly differentiated—a centre of excellence in ENT for the state of Georgia, but its dedication to the specialism has enabled it to drive down costs to a level well below those of general hospitals—and despite each of its five ENT specialist doctors earning over $1m, from a turnover of $27m.

Keep your ears pricked as ENTI looks to neighboring states...

Grouping into strategic alternatives

By now you should have a whole range of profit growth options. The danger is that it may look like a laundry list.

It should help to group them into two or three strategic alternatives. Each will represent a defined and coherent strategy for bridging the strategic gap in this business. One alternative may reflect investment primarily in one segment, another may reflect investment spread across a combination of segments and business-wide processes.

They should be mutually exclusive—you can follow one or another, but not both (or all). You can follow just the one alternative.

Grouping into strategic alternatives makes evaluation more manageable. Rather than evaluating 20 profit growth options, you will be evaluating two or three strategic alternatives.

Making the strategic investment decision

You have drawn up two or three strategic alternatives aimed at bridging the strategic gap in your business. They were mutually exclusive, so you can only take one of them. How do you evaluate them and select the best?

The answer is straightforward in theory. You should choose the alternative that gives you *the highest return for the lowest risk.*

How you get there is not quite so straightforward. There is a spectrum of methods, ranging from the dangerously complex—real option valuation—to the dangerously simple—impact on earnings.

In the interests of KISS, you may opt for the payback method. It has its faults, many of them, but its virtue is its simplicity. As long as you use it with care, this method should for the most part do the job.—see Figure 2.9.

Work out the cost of the investment, say £I. Assess the annual benefits from the investment, namely the difference between the extra cash inflow (from revenues) and the extra cash out-

KISS tip

The financial consequences of making the wrong strategic investment decision may be severe. If you are in doubt, get some help with the financial analysis. A few thousand bucks for advice up front might save you tens even hundreds of thousands down the line.

Figure 2.9 **The payback approach to evaluating strategic alternatives**

	Unit	Strategic alternatives		
		A	B	C
Financial benefits				
Investment costs = I	$000			
Average annual cash benefits over 5 years = B	$000/ year			
Payback = I /B	Years			
Total cash benefits over 5 years = TB = Bx5	$000			
Net benefits = TB - I	$000			
Risk	L/M/H			
Non-financial benefits		*	*	* ....
		*	*	* ....
Non-financial disbenefits		*	*	* ....
		*	*	* ....

flow (from expenses) generated each year as a result of the investment. If the annual benefits are different each year, take their average over the first five years, £B/year. Divide B into I, and this gives you the 'payback', the number of years taken for the cash costs of the investment to be recouped.

If payback is *four years or less*, that could well be a sound investment. But don't jump on it. Work out the payback on the other strategic alternatives as well. They may have an even lower payback.

If you believe your investment is going to give you a longer-term advantage, and could last all of ten years, then an investment with a longer payback may still be beneficial. You might give serious consideration to an investment with a payback of six to seven years. It'll be riskier, of course, because all sorts of things could happen to your competitive position over time.

Next work out the 'net benefits' of the strategic alternative, the total benefits over the five years less the investment cost.

The most promising alternative should be the one with the

highest net benefits and with an acceptable payback.

Note that the alternative with the fastest payback is not necessarily the best—net benefits may be too small, even though they are the most rapidly achieved. But if the alternative with the fastest payback is not mutually exclusive with the one that has the highest net benefits, perhaps you could do both?

Now for the caveats:

- Do not take account of the cash already invested in an alternative—this is history, so-called 'sunken costs'; only account for new cash that needs to be injected.

- Remember the time value of money—cash flows in Year 5 are not worth as much to you today as those in Year 1, so beware lumpy cash flows.

- The payback method isn't kind to those alternatives with a longer gestation period, with cash generated mainly beyond the payback period.

- Don't forget your non-financial goals, which may be affected by one or more of the alternatives.

- Above all, don't forget risk—it is most unlikely that each alternative will carry the same degree of risk.

If your strategic investment decision is complex, and especially if benefits are late developing, do it properly through discounted cash flow analysis. If you don't feel comfortable with that, engage a specialist.

The strategic investment decision is seldom clear cut. The financials are often hard to evaluate and even then there may be a trade-off between financial return, risk, and meeting non-financial goals. The decision is yours.

Bridging the gap for a startup

Earlier in this chapter we targeted the gap between your competitive position upon launch of your venture and that of where you need to be three years out—by when your competi-

> **KISS tip**
>
> For a startup, you have two choices of generic strategy: low cost or differentiated. One or the other. Period.

tive advantage must have become or is due to become sustainable.

But how to get there?

There is nothing special here about a startup. In bridging the strategic gap, the process is the same as for an established business:

- Confirm your generic strategy—low cost or differentiated; don't opt for a focused strategy or you'll run the risk of being stuck in the middle—medium cost, medium differentiation, a recipe for business failure; a focused strategy is a luxury afforded to a more mature company with economies of scale; for a startup, be low cost or differentiated and do not waiver.

- Shaping profit growth options—crafting a set of initiatives to bridge the gap in the segments to be invested in, including those needed to protect yourself against competitive response; for a startup, of course, all segments are new and to be invested in—there are, by definition, as yet, no segments for holding or exit; group them into two or three strategic alternatives.

- Evaluate the alternatives—perhaps using the payback method described above.

To reiterate, to survive your launch you must have a distinct competitive advantage—with a low cost or differentiated strategy. To survive three to five years out, that competitive advantage must have become sustainable.

Figure 2.10 Creating competitive advantage

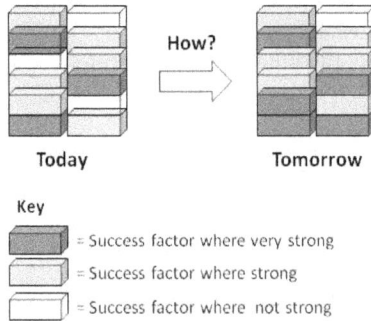

To summarize this chapter, as in Figure 2.10:

- *Track your competitive position*: how are you placed?
- *Target the gap*: where should you be placed?
- *Bridge the gap*: how should you get there?

But there's one more wrinkle: in your strategy to bridge the gap, what are the risks?

3 Managing

risk

\\\\

The biggest risk is not taking any risk... In a world that is changing really quickly, the only strategy that is guaranteed to fail is not taking risks, Mark Zuckerberg

Risk is all around you. As in your personal life, so too with business. The trick is to understand it and contain it.

Each aspect of strategy development is subject to risk:

- Market demand may take a dip, wholly beyond your control.

- A competitor may steamroller into your market, regardless of the financial consequences.

- A key customer is taken over and you are ditched as a supplier.

- Your new product launch may flop.

- Your distribution partner may go under.

But before you give up the ghost, think on this: each risk may have a corresponding opportunity, viz:

- Market demand may receive a boost, again wholly beyond your control.

- A competitor may withdraw from your market or go under.

- A key customer makes an acquisition and invites you to supply both.

- Your new product launch succeeds beyond expectations.

- Your distribution partner expands and introduces new customers to you.

Phew! Life ain't so bad after all…

It is all about balance and judgment. And process.

Assessing the balance of risk and opportunity

Here is what you do. Go through each part of the strategy development process again, especially the sections on market
demand and industry competition, and pull out what seem to
be the main risks and opportunities.

Assess them from two perspectives:

- How likely are they to take place?—low, medium or
  high.
- If they do occur, how large an impact will they have?—
  low, medium or large.

Now isolate what we shall term the 'big' risks and opportunities, as defined by those where:

- Likelihood of occurrence is medium (or high) and impact is high.
- Likelihood of occurrence is high and impact is medium
  (or high).

You are now ready for these big risks and opportunities to be
compared and assessed.

I first created the Suns & Clouds chart in the early 1990s.
Since then I've seen it reproduced in various forms in reports
by my consulting competitors. They say imitation is the sin-
cerest form of flattery, but I still kick myself that I didn't
copyright it back then!

The reason it keeps getting pinched is that it works. It manages to encapsulate in one chart conclusions on the relative
importance of all the main strategic issues. It shows, diagram-
matically and visually, whether the opportunities surpass the
risks. Or vice-versa. In short, in one chart, it tells you whether

Figure 3.1 **The Suns & Clouds chart**

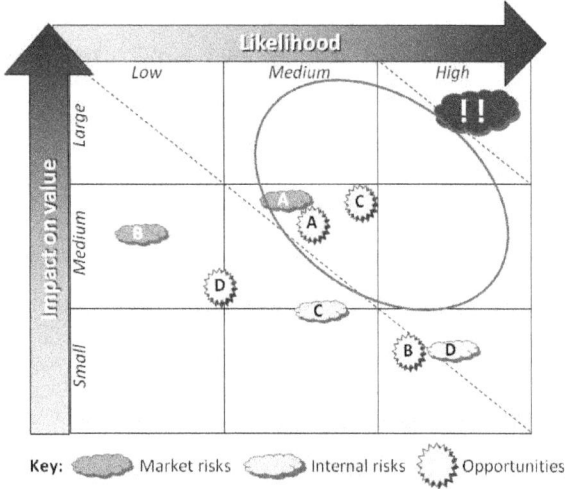

Key: Market risks   Internal risks   Opportunities

your strategy is backable. Or not.

The chart (Figure 3.1) forces you to view each risk (and opportunity) from two perspectives: how likely it is to happen, and how big an impact it would have if it did. You don't need to quantify the impact, but instead have some idea of the notional, *relative* impact of each issue on the value of the firm.

In the chart, risks are represented as clouds, opportunities as suns. For each risk (and opportunity), you need to place it in the appropriate position on the chart taking into account both

KISS tip

Take care with the individual probabilities. It is human nature to overinflate expectations for opportunities and downplay those for risks.

Over-optimism may help in team motivation but is most unhelpful in strategy development.

its likelihood and impact.

The chart tells you two main things about how backable is your strategy: whether there are any extraordinary risks (or opportunities), and whether the overall balance of risk and opportunity is favorable.

Extraordinary risk

Take a look at the top right-hand corner of the chart. There's a heavy thundercloud in there, with two exclamation marks. That's a risk that is both very likely and very big. It's a show-stopper risk. If you find one of them, your strategy is unback-able.

The closer a cloud gets to that thundercloud, the worse news it is. Risks that hover around the diagonal (from the top left to the bottom right corners) can be handled, as long as they are balanced by opportunities. But as soon as a cloud starts creep-ing toward that thundercloud, for example to around where opportunity C is placed, that's when you should start to worry.

But imagine a bright shining sun in the spot where that thun-dercloud is. That's terrific news, and you'll have suitors clam-bering over each other to back you.

The balance of risk

In general there's no showstopper risk. The main purpose of the Suns & Clouds chart will then be to present the *balance* of risk and opportunity. Do the opportunities surpass the risks? Given the overall picture, are the suns more favorably placed than the clouds? Or do the clouds overshadow the suns?

The way to assess a Suns & Clouds chart is to look first at the general area above the diagonal and in the direction of the thundercloud. This is the area covered in Figure 3.1 by the parabola. Any risk (or opportunity) there is worthy of note: it's at least reasonably likely to occur *and* would have at least a reasonable impact.

Those risks and opportunities below the diagonal are less important. They are either of low to medium likelihood *and* of low to medium impact. Or they're not big enough, or not likely enough, to be of major concern.

Take a look at the pattern of suns and clouds in your chart around the area of the parabola. The closer each sun or cloud to the thundercloud, the more important it is. If the pattern of suns seems better placed than the pattern of clouds, your strategy may be backable.

In the chart above, there are two clouds and two suns above the diagonal. But risk D lies outside the parabola. The best placed is opportunity B. Risk A and opportunity A more or less balance each other out, likewise other risks and opportunities. Opportunity B seems distinctly clear of the pack. The opportunities seem to surpass the risks. The strategy looks backable.

One of the best features of the Suns & Clouds chart is that it can be made dynamic. If the balance of risk and opportunity shown on the chart is unfavorable, you may be able to do something about it—and the chart will show this clearly.

For every risk, there are mitigating factors. Many, including those relating to market demand and competition (the darker clouds in Figure 3.1), will be beyond your control. Those relating to your firm's competitive position, however, are within your power to influence. They may indeed be an integral part of your emergent strategy.

Likewise, your strategy may improve the likelihood of achieving a key opportunity on the chart, thereby shifting the sun to the right.

Risk mitigation or opportunity enhancement in the Suns & Clouds chart can be illuminated with arrows and target signs. They'll show where your firm should aim for and remind you that it's a target. Your strategy should improve the overall balance of risk and opportunity in your firm.

You can use the Suns & Clouds chart in so many situations. It was designed for use in transactions such as acquisitions, alliances and investments, but it is just as useful in project appraisal, strategy review (as here) or even in career develop-

> **KISS tip**
>
> Don't worry if your Suns & Clouds chart doesn't make that much sense initially. This chart changes with further thought and discussion. *Always.* Arguably its greatest virtue is its stimulus to discussion. It provokes amendment.
>
> Remember, you cannot be exact in this chart. Nor do you need to be. It is a pictorial representation of risk and opportunity, designed to give you a *feel* for the balance of risk and opportunity in your strategy.

ment and change. It might even have been useful in deciding whether or not to have backed Britney (see Figure 3.2).

What about highly improbable but potentially catastrophic risks, you might ask? And those which seem explicable even justifiable only in retrospect, termed 'Black Swans' by Nassim Nicholas Taleb—like the 2008 financial meltdown? The chart deals with them too.

In the fall of 2001, my colleagues and I were advising a client on whether to invest in a company involved in airport operations. After the first week of work, we produced an interim report and a first-cut Suns & Clouds chart. In the top left-hand corner box, we placed a risk entitled 'major air incident'. We were thinking of a serious air crash that might lead to the prolonged grounding of a common class of aircraft. It seemed unlikely, but would have a very large impact if it happened.

9/11 came just a few days later. We never envisaged anything so devastating, so inconceivably evil, but at least we had alerted our client to the extreme risks involved in the air industry. The deal was renegotiated and completed successfully.

Britney does it again

Who do you think was the highest paid woman in the music industry in 2012? No, not Beyoncé, not even Taylor, but Britney! The schoolgirl sensation from the late 1990s was back at the top with $68m.

Britney stormed onto the music scene with *Baby One More Time*. The voice was good enough, as was the song, but it was the positioning of this 17 year old that sealed the deal—with the video designed overtly to fuel the fantasies of every schoolboy and the aspirations of every schoolgirl—including my two. She became their goddess and, as soon as Britney brought out her first fragrance, Santa duly obliged.

History may tell us that this video marked a seminal moment in the sad but inexorable process of the sexualization of schoolkids, but it did the trick for Britney. She became the bestselling teenage artist ever and by 2002 Forbes magazine was rating her as the world's most powerful celebrity.

But in early 2004 came the first signs that something was amiss. She married a childhood sweetheart in Las Vegas then annulled it within three days. She attended the Kabbalah sect of her role model, Madonna. She became engaged to a dancer and opened up their lives in a three month reality show. They had two children, but sadly divorced within two years.

She became in her own words an "emotional wreck". She partied heavily with the likes of Paris Hilton, flirting with paparazzi and flagrantly displaying her absence of underwear. She shaved off all her hair. She checked in and out of drug rehabilitation centers. She lost custody of her children to her ex-husband. By early 2008 she was hospitalized and put under the conservatorship of her father.

If you were a music industry mogul in mid-2008, would

Figure 3.2 **Would you have backed Britney in 2008?**

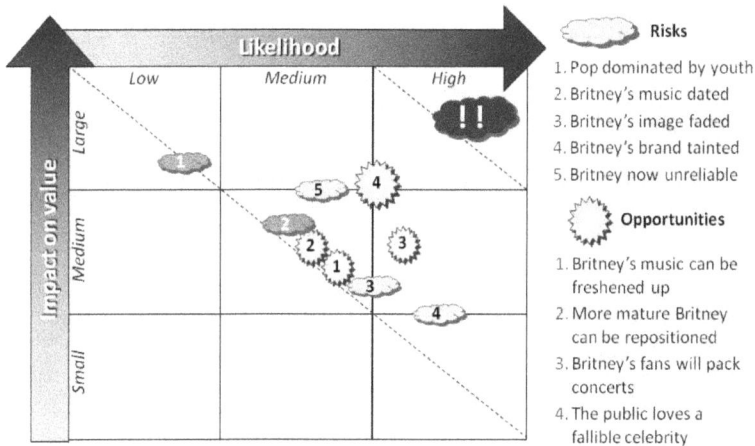

Likelihood

| Low | Medium | High |

Impact on value: Large / Medium / Small

Risks
1. Pop dominated by youth
2. Britney's music dated
3. Britney's image faded
4. Britney's brand tainted
5. Britney now unreliable

Opportunities
1. Britney's music can be freshened up
2. More mature Britney can be repositioned
3. Britney's fans will pack concerts
4. The public loves a fallible celebrity

you have backed Britney? The risks were huge. She had been a teen star like none other, but that was yesterday. At 27 she was passé, troubled, and unreliable. Her looks had lost their freshness, her body was turning maternal, her voice remained unexceptional. How could she compete with a Beyoncé?

Let's look at her Suns & Clouds—see Figure 3.2.

It wouldn't have looked too good. Risks and opportunities seem more or less balanced out—with Britney's dated music, fading image, tarnished brand, and unreliable character balanced by opportunities to freshen up the music, reposition her as more mature and to rely on the legion of diehard fans to show up when her concert comes to town, again like my daughters!

But one opportunity steals the show. The public loves a fallible celebrity. And any news is good news. As long as she could pull herself together, and perform when required, countering that risk #5, that opportunity, sun #4, should shine through to success.

And, yes, four years later, oops, she did it again and hit us, baby, one more time.

Containing risk

There is one further use for your Suns & Clouds chart. It can highlight the scope for containing areas of risk in your strategy.

Strip out all the suns from your chart, leaving just the clouds, and super-impose four boxes, carefully located, containing the words 'accept', 'reduce', 'transfer', and 'avoid'—see Figure 3.3.

Your four basic strategies for managing risk then are:

- Where at all possible, AVOID the big risks—if it's an internal risk, don't do it; if it's a market risk, withdraw.

- Where it's not possible to avoid a big risk, TRANSFER it to your insurers.

- REDUCE the medium risks through limitation, for example through greater storage for supplies or more sophisticated systems and data back-up.

- ACCEPT the small risks.

Make sure though that the exercise doesn't grind you down. The trouble with many risk management tools is that they can be unbalanced. The beauty of the Suns & Clouds chart is that it acknowledges risk, but balances it with opportunity. A purely risk management chart like that of Figure 3.3 has no such balance and may seem like unremitting gloom.

Figure 3.3 **Containing risk**

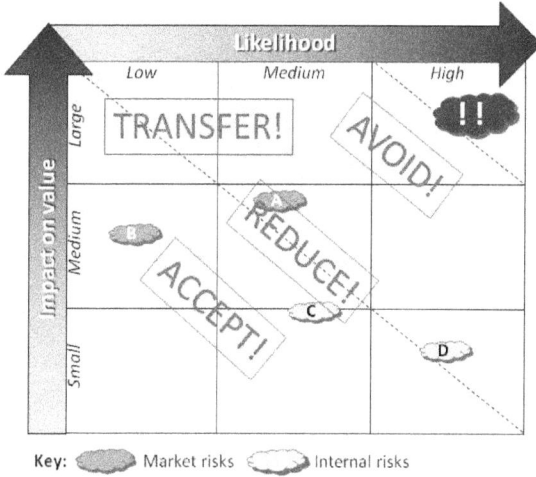

Key: Market risks   Internal risks

Risks do need to be managed, but risk containment must not become obsessive. It mustn't get in the way of developing a robust, challenging, value-enhancing strategy for your business.

Conclusion

"

You have brains in your head. You have feet in your shoes. You can steer yourself in any direction you choose.", Dr Seuss

You now have a strategy, a KISSTRATEGY, to guide your firm to the next level.

Your firm is now far better equipped for the future than it was before.

Michael Porter wrote that "the company without a strategy is willing to try anything".

Not yours. It will have direction. You will be facing the future with a strategy which will maximize the chances of achieving your goals.

You will have the strategy you need for your business to succeed.

VAUGHAN EVANS

Appendix: the Strategy Pyramid

The Strategy Pyramid

Source: Vaughan Evans, *Key Strategy Tools*, Pearson, 2012

This book has applied the KISS principle to strategy development. In earlier books, such as *Key Strategy Tools* (FT Publishing, 2012), I set out a more comprehensive strategy development process termed the Strategy Pyramid. This appendix briefly reconciles the two.

The Strategy Pyramid (see Figure A.1 above) consists of nine building blocks:

> 1: Knowing your business
>
> 2: Setting goals and objectives
>
> 3: Forecasting market demand
>
> 4: Gauging industry competition
>
> 5: Tracking competitive advantage
>
> 6: Targeting the strategic gap
>
> 7: Bridging the gap with business strategy
>
> 8: Bridging the gap with corporate strategy
>
> 9: Addressing risk and opportunity

It is a logical, coherent and proven approach to strategy development. But it has one defect. It has nine building blocks. Some people find it hard to remember nine of anything. Psychologists tell us that three is the number of items that the human brain can best process and recall.

So the first step in applying the KISS principle to strategy development had to be to reduce the nine blocks to three stages. This turned out to be quite simple—see Figure A.2.

Blocks 1 and 2 are really preparatory steps, getting ready for the strategy process. So they can be put to one side.

Blocks 3 and 4 represent the assessing of demand and supply in the market, the 'micro-economy' in which your firm operates.

Blocks 5 through to 8 represent the building of your firm's enduring competitive advantage—though Block 8 on corporate strategy (for a multi-business company) becomes redun-

Figure A.2 **From 'Strategy Pyramid' to KISSTRATEGY**

The Strategy Pyramid	KISSTRATEGY
Block 1: Knowing your business Block 2: Setting goals and objectives	[Getting ready]
Block 3: Forecasting market demand Block 4: Gauging industry competition	**1. Understanding the market**
Block 5: Tracking competitive position Block 6: Targeting the strategic gap Block 7: Bridging the gap with business strategy [Block 8: Bridging the gap with corporate strategy]	**2. Creating competitive advantage**
Block 9: Addressing risk and opportunity	**3. Managing risk**

dant in a book designed for the small business reader.

And Block 9 is about balancing strategic risk and opportunity and checking that the risks are manageable.

So there we have it: the three essential parts of strategy development and KISSTRATEGY:

* Understanding the market

* Creating competitive advantage

* Managing risk

It is no coincidence that these three parts satisfy the perspectives of three distinct sets of stakeholders, each of whose hats I have worn at different stages of my career.

As an economist, strategy needs to be harmonious with the market in which the firm operates, the so-called 'microeconomy'—Part 1. As a business strategist, strategy must focus on creating an enduring competitive advantage—Part 2. And finally, as a financier, strategy has to address and contain risk—Part 3.

Put the three parts together and you have a simple yet comprehensive approach to strategy development—and one that aligns the strategist with both the economist and the financier.

This is KISSTRATEGY.

Read on...

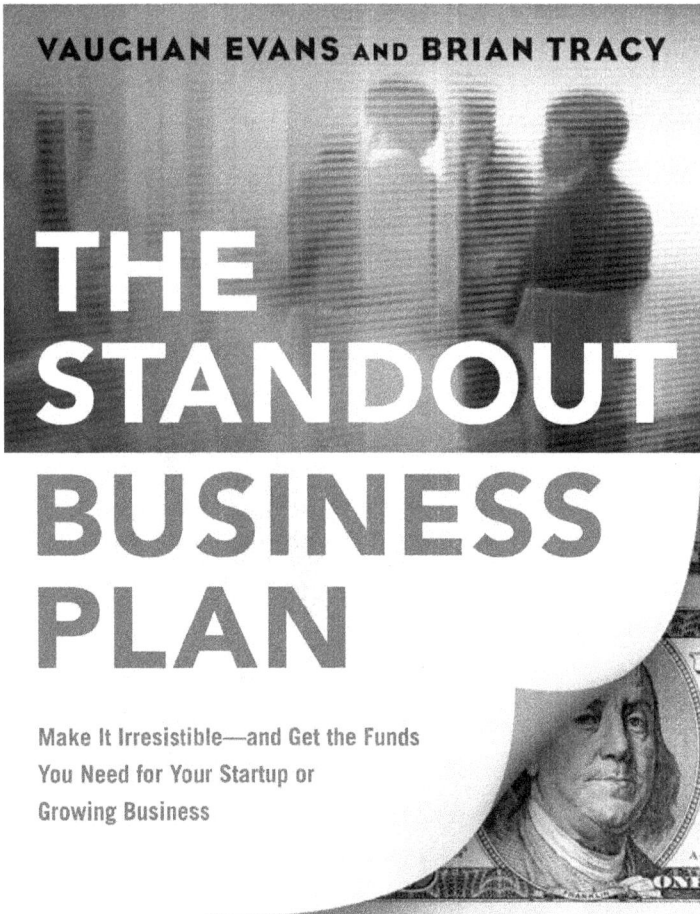

VAUGHAN EVANS AND BRIAN TRACY

THE STANDOUT BUSINESS PLAN

Make It Irresistible—and Get the Funds
You Need for Your Startup or
Growing Business

And...

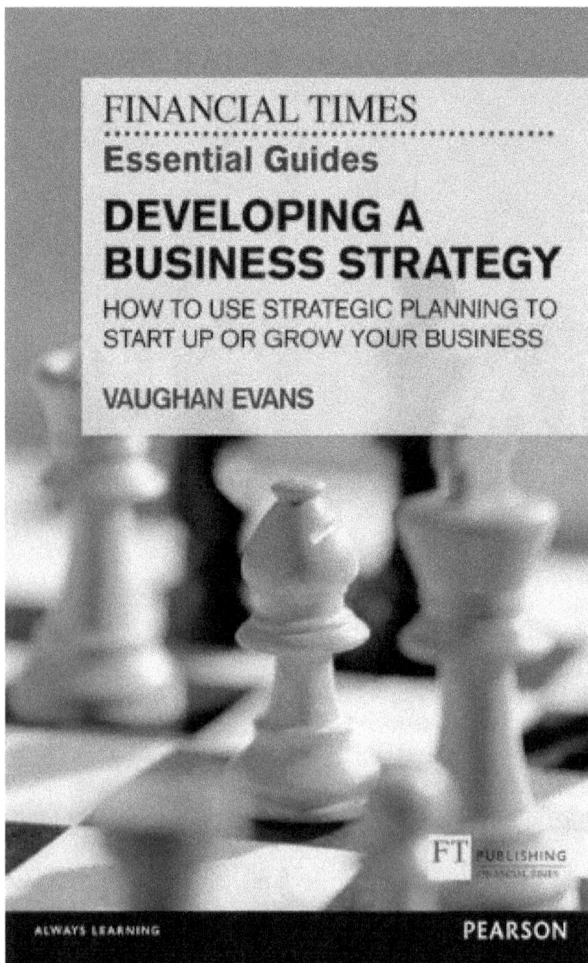

O r...

Key Strategy Tools

The 80+ Tools Every
Manager Needs to Know

Vaughan Evans

FT PUBLISHING
FINANCIAL TIMES

VAUGHAN EVANS